Minding the Self

Many people have an aptitude for religious experience and spirituality but do not know how to develop this or take it further. Modern societies offer little assistance, and traditional religions are overly preoccupied with their own organizational survival. *Minding the Self: Jungian meditations on contemporary spirituality* offers suggestions for individual spiritual development in our modern and post-modern times. Here, Murray Stein argues that C.G. Jung and depth psychology provide guidance and the foundation for a new kind of modern spirituality.

Murray Stein explores the problem of spirituality within the cultural context of modernity and offers a way forward without relapsing into traditional or mythological modes of consciousness. Chapters work towards finding the proper vessel for contemporary spirituality and dealing with the ethical issues that crop up along the way. Stein shows how it is an individual path but not an isolationist one, often using many resources borrowed from a variety of religious traditions: it is a way of symbol, dream and experiences of the numinous with hints of transcendence as these come into personal awareness.

Minding the Self: Jungian meditations on contemporary spirituality uses research from a wide variety of fields, such as dream-work and the neuroscience of the sleeping brain, clinical experience in Jungian psychoanalysis, anthropology, ethics, Zen Buddhism, Jung's writings and the recently published *Red Book*. It will be of interest to psychoanalysts, Jungian scholars, undergraduates, graduate and post-graduate students and anyone with an interest in modern spirituality.

Murray Stein is a training and supervising analyst at the International School of Analytical Psychology, Zurich, Switzerland. He is the author of many articles and books.

Minding the Self

Jungian meditations on contemporary spirituality

Murray Stein

 Routledge
Taylor & Francis Group

LONDON AND NEW YORK

First published 2014
by Routledge
27 Church Road, Hove, East Sussex BN3 2FA

and by Routledge
711 Third Avenue, New York, NY 10017

Routledge is an imprint of the Taylor & Francis Group, an informa business

British Library Cataloguing in Publication Data
A catalogue record for this book is available from the British Library.

Library of Congress Cataloging-in-Publication Data
Stein, Murray, 1943-
Minding the self : Jungian meditations on contemporary spirituality/Murray Stein. – First Edition.
pages cm
1. Jung, C. G. (Carl Gustav), 1875–1961. 2. Psychoanalysis and religion. 3. Spirituality. I. Title.
BF175.4.R44S7394 2014
150.19'54–dc23
2013037164

ISBN: 978-0-415-37785-0 (hbk)
ISBN: 978-0-415-37784-3 (pbk)
ISBN: 978-1-315-79763-2 (ebk)

Typeset in Times New Roman
by Deer Park Productions

Contents

15 Minding the self   111

    References   127
    Index   130

Acknowledgements

This book has come into being in bits and pieces over a period of time, many chapters first taking other forms and appearing as articles in various journals or chapters in books. Each has its own story. I have worked to shape them into a coherent series of what I now think of as Jungian meditations. Parts of:

Chapter One appeared in the *Journal of Analytical Psychology*, 3:2007 as 'Of Text and Contexts';
Chapter Two in the *Journal of Analytical Psychology* 3:2008 as '"Divinity Expresses the Self..." An Investigation';
Chapter Three in *The Guild of Pastoral Psychology Pamphlet* No. 278, 2001 as 'A Changing God Image: What Does It Mean?';
Chapter Four in *Symbolic Life 2009*, *Spring Journal* 82: 2009 as 'Symbol as Psychic Transformer';
Chapter Six in *The Idea of the Numinous* (Eds Ann Casement and David Tacey), Routledge, 2006 as 'On the Importance of Numinous Experience in the Alchemy of Individuation';
Chapter Eight in *Spirituality in Depth* (Ed. Avis Clendenen) Chiron Publications, 2002, as 'The Reality of the Soul';
Chapter Nine in *Analytical Psychology: Contemporary Perspectives in Jungian Analysis* (Eds Joseph Cambray and Linda Carter), Routledge, 2004, as 'Spiritual and Religious Aspects of Modern Analysis';
Chapter Eleven in *Initiation: The Reality of a Living Archetype* (Eds Thomas Kirsch, Virginia Beane Rutter and Thomas Singer), Routledge, 2007 as 'On Modern Initiation into the Spiritual – a Psychological View';
Chapter Twelve in *The Allure of Gnosticism* (Ed. Robert Segal), Open Court, 1995 as 'The Gnostic Critique, Past and Present'.

I have vastly changed the previously published essays to incorporate more recent thoughts and insights and to relate them to one another in this text. Also, in putting this work together, new themes emerged that were not as clear to me when the parts were shaped previously, and these have been woven into the fabric of the book.

I would like to thank Kate Hawes of Routledge for her patient support throughout the slow process of completing this book, also Andrew Samuels for his initial encouragement. For permission to use the Ten Ox-Herding Pictures by Shuhbun, my profound thanks to Shokukuji-Temple and the assistance of Professor Mari Yoshikawa of Gakushin University in Tokyo. Many friends have commented on the chapters, for which I am grateful, and especially to my wife, Jan Stein, for her several helpful critical readings of the entire text.

Grateful acknowledgement is made to the following for permission to reprint: Excerpts from Jung, C.G., *Collected Works of C.G. Jung*, 1977, Princeton University Press, reprinted by permission of Princeton University Press.

Excerpts from *The Red Book* by C.G. Jung, edited by Sonu Shamdasani, translated by Mark Kyburz, John Peck, and Sonu Shamdasani. Copyright 2009, the Foundation of the Works of C.G. Jung. Translation 2009 by Mark Kyburz, John Peck, and Sonu Shamdasani. Used by permission of W.W. Norton & Company, Inc.

Excerpts from *Memories, Dreams, Reflections* by C.G. Jung, edited by Aniela Jaffe, translated by Richard and Clara Winston, translation copyright 1961, 1962, 1963 and renewed 1989, 1990, 1991 by Random House, Inc. Used by permission of Pantheon Books, a division of Random House, Inc.

Any third party use of this material, outside of this publication, is prohibited. Interested parties must apply directly to Random House, Inc. for permission.

The Ten Ox-Herding Pictures by Shuhbun reproduced by permission of Shokokuji-Temple, Kyoto, Japan.

Introduction

One morning I stepped softly into the back of a traditional Catholic cathedral in Braga, Portugal. It was a bright Sunday in July 2012, and the interior was dark so it took a few moments to adjust my eyesight. A ceremonially-clad priest was reciting the Mass. It felt like I had stepped back into the Middle Ages. The church was not exactly packed, but it was not empty either and considerably fuller than one finds churches on a Sunday morning these days in Switzerland where I live. The people here were clearly intent on the religious service at hand. The well-maintained sanctuary was filled to the brim with images, statues, and symbols that spoke of Christ's life and sacrificial crucifixion. Arching impressively high above the altar was a dramatic three-dimensional reconstruction of Calvary, with Christ in the center dying magnificently, while below and around him all the other biblical life-size figures in the story were arranged as if for a film set. I could see that most of the people in the congregation were of simple background and origin, with a light smattering of tourists in casual dress among them. The group of worshippers looked to be equally divided between men and women and, I guessed, aged between 30 and 80. All seemed affixed by the words coming from the altar as the priest invoked the Divine in the age-old phrases of the Roman Catholic Mass.

This is not my religion, I thought quietly to myself. I am a lifelong Protestant, trained to think critically, oriented to the Word and not to icons, and largely unmoved by traditional Catholic symbols and rituals. I have to recognize that the people here occupy another world, I said to myself, and they dwell in it at least momentarily with religious awe and wonder, or perhaps with a lesser degree of participation but certainly with devotion and respect. This is obvious in their devout demeanor. I have no idea who they are or what is going through their minds, but I can see in their faces and body language evidence of religious feeling. They have entered a symbolic world, and they occupy it without irony or critical attitudes lurking in the back of their minds. They live in the same chronological period of history as I do, but culturally we are centuries apart. I am indelibly modern. I cannot go where they are, although I can imagine and appreciate their worldview at least to some extent. But their symbols are not mine.

After a few minutes, I stepped out of the dark church and back into the sunlight. The whole interior space felt somewhat claustrophobic to me, even if it invited participants into a supernatural world. There was little room for thinking freely there. Besides, I stand most comfortably with my Protestant forebears, Zwingli and Calvin, who stripped the cathedrals of their statues and images and offered the Word instead – intellect, abstraction, meaning based on ideas and not influenced by painted images, physical rituals, colorful windows and sculpted forms. In the Reformation, thinking overruled artfulness and intuition allied itself with feeling to produce a strict ethical attitude. The result was grey and plain, and the Protestant world became logical and abstract, eventually yielding to modernity with its mathematics and science. Today the words spoken sermonically in most of the Protestant churches I know of are banal and the ideas largely outdated. The word "God" has become devoid of vital associations and left at stories from the biblical text. This is the current crisis in biblical religion. Token shards of past meaning are what remain in the churches, leading to nothing more than some minor quiverings of nostalgia.

This is modernity, too. Modernity casts aside symbol, myth, religious objects, and meaning-generating images in favor of doubt, the agnostic shrug, and scientific reserve. We wait for research to give us answers to our questions, and such answers as we get from the laboratory are never final and always leave us with an expectation of further modifications or even reversals. In the modern mind, there remains no room to entertain the notion of an invisible, supernatural world beyond the visible one. The natural world is all there is, and science provides the means for exploring it.

However, this does not mean that one cannot resonate to ancient myth, even emotionally, be it Greek, Egyptian, Hindu or any other from the vast selection of the world's belief systems. Some modern people have, in fact, taken great interest in considering ancient myth as marvelous, even fundamental, metaphors for human existence. Mythopoetics has bloomed in many quarters. Still one is left wondering: if we read the great books of history and study the many mythologies of the world in our amazing up-to-date libraries and on the worldwide web, do we experience them as numinous and convincing? This requires a great leap of imagination, which is suspect in our modern materialist time zone. It is often observed, too, that the themes of myth thoroughly penetrate our contemporary storytelling and media, but they do not generate faith or belief. They entertain. Novels, films, poems, or the latest TV series are fully capable of arousing strong emotion, but they rarely leave us with an experience of numinosity that transforms our lives. They may flicker with numinosity but they do not sustain. They are momentary pleasures. Mythopoetic imagination can generate powerful waves of emotion, but they are more distractions from the serious business of living our lives than transformative encounters with the Divine. Modernity makes do without big symbols and symbolic meanings of the type that religions provided in previous times. The need for "salvation", for instance, rings few bells today, unless it is translated into social and economic terms. There is no sense of "soul" and "spirit" in modernity, even if creativity and innovation are highly prized for their economic value. Those of us who are imbued with this culture may struggle mightily but most often completely in vain to find a way to attain to what the ancients and the religious traditions lived fully and without self-reflective consciousness, namely a symbolic life.

I once attended a highly charged and magnificently enacted dramatization of a version of the play *Agamemnon* from the *Oresteia* by Aeschylus, whose point was to bring the audience into direct contact with the wrath of the Earth Goddess, Gaia, who is objecting violently to the abuses being visited upon her by our present lack of ecological sensitivity. Gaia's violent screams were shattering in their ferocity, and they frightened me and others in the audience to the point that we were momentarily convinced that we must at all costs attend to Earth's needs or be condemned to relentless, unforgiving punishment. Leaving the theater, I was deeply impressed by the power of the presentation and its message. Later, though, I began to wonder about Gaia. She is a metaphor, I thought, and the authors of the play are employing this image and the power of language to make their political views heard on an emotional level. But will politicians and scientists and hard-nosed business people leap into action at Gaia's cries from the stage and deliver their unanimous consent that the Earth as they know it, a geological entity, is indeed doing what Gaia's screams indicate? Is the Earth really "punishing" us for our sins against "the mother"? In a manner of speaking, metaphorically taken, yes, maybe. But this is a constructed human metaphor after all, a product of the playwright's imagination and driven by emotions, largely of fear and guilt. Can we take something like this seriously when we no longer believe in Gaia as a deity? What is the source of this message? Does it come from the Beyond or from the here and now? Don't we have to rely on measurement and rational investigation instead of ramped-up emotion generated by theater to discover the truth and to act?

So I ask myself: Is there still a way that symbols, even God images, can be convincing and sustain a sense of meaning in modernity? Metaphors exist aplenty in film, literature, and art, and they pass before our eyes continuously, but they leave little behind except the memory of an emotional experience and perhaps a few ideas that can be gleaned and abstracted from them. Metaphors help us to think, no doubt, but do they offer direction and are they reliable?

They can also interfere with clear thinking. Science is deeply suspicious of them. Perhaps we need to make do with rationality and sober calculation, and to use technology itself to tame the excesses of technological culture. To prevent the destruction of nature we need science, not symbols. But is science enough to live by? What about our need for meaning? Neither metaphors nor science seem to be sufficient.

In this work, I want to maintain a tension of opposites that is endemic in modernity. On one side of this strained pair of contraries stand the metaphoric and the religious tendencies in our very nature, which cannot be dismissed without deleterious results; on the other side and pulling in the opposite direction is our strong cultural preference for critical thinking, abstract formulation, scientific evidence and iconoclasm (no images please!). Modernity leans toward the iconoclastic and the logical, of course, but it proves to be impossible to think, speak and indeed to live without image, metaphor and symbol. The modern tilt toward science in this tension is reflected in the contemporary hierarchical arrangement of the natural sciences and the humanities in university faculties, with the social sciences trying valiantly but mostly fruitlessly to offer themselves as important cousins of the natural sciences. However, on the fringes of modern societies and mostly out of sight of university departments, there continues to exist a mighty pull toward spirituality and the transcendent that resists quantification and logical analysis and insists on its own vision of reality. This insistence on a space for spirituality does not disappear even in the most modern and materialistic of cultures. In fact, scientific surveys indicate that there is a resurgence of interest in all kinds of spirituality in the modern world today. David Tacey even speaks of a "spirituality revolution" in our times and "the emergence of contemporary spirituality" (Tacey 2004) and locates pockets of evidence for his thesis in many areas of modern societies.

In modernity, and now as well in post-modernity, we have to live at once with and without symbols of transcendence and the spiritual. It is a subtle balancing act. We have to live with them because they come to us spontaneously and without special invitation, as visitations of the numinous. But even as we hold them in mind we must also think our way through and beyond them, in other words make them conscious and integrate them. This is a tension to be lived and maintained. What I am advocating, in summary, is an individual path to spirituality that is grounded in personal experiences and lived by reflecting upon them using a psychological perspective. It exists outside of all religious organizations and structures. I will speak of this way of attending to the spiritual as "minding the self."

Chapter I

"New wine needs new skins"

To expand on my theme of minding the self, I will make use throughout this book of C.G. Jung's life and work. I do not apologize for this since my intention is not to make Jung into a hero and set him up as an ideal. I will use his biography and writings to add flesh to the bones of the discussion. This is nothing more than a way of speaking about the spiritual dilemma that faces many modern people because Jung exemplified it so exquisitely and wrote about it so fulsomely throughout his long life. His brilliant attempts to resolve the collective problem of spirituality within a culture of modernity, on a lived and a theoretical level, are of use for advancing the discussion even if they do not provide all the answers one might desire. Jung took note of the spiritual discontent in modern society and tried to do more than merely diagnose it. He tried to relieve it. It turns out to be quite a radical treatment.

By now it is well known that throughout his life Jung was continuously engaged, in one way or another, in a conscious dialogue with religion, most intensely of course with his own background religious tradition, Christianity. This is made clear in the late autobiographical work, *Memories, Dreams, Reflections*, where he recalls his childhood in a Protestant parsonage, his failed discussions with his Swiss Reformed pastor father, Paul Jung, and his early and late struggles with faith and belief. Unlike Freud, Jung did not identify fully with the Enlightenment and the supreme value of reason and positivist science to the detriment of feeling and especially intuition. In this respect, he leaned in the direction of German Romanticism and its high regard for myth, symbol and mystery. The intellect, Jung often said, was a trickster and could lead one away from a full consideration of reality, especially psychic reality. Moreover, he felt himself to stand in partial continuity at least with Christianity, the tradition of his forebears, even if he did not claim belief in its dogmatic formulations. In his deepest registers, Jung responded to life as a *homo religiosus*, a man keenly attuned to spirituality even though he stood apart from religious organizations. He had a strong sense of what Max Weber memorably named "religious musicality", which Weber also noted is generally absent from modernity. In a sense, Jung can be seen even as a throw-back to the Middle Ages, but with the difference that he was educated and trained as a modern scientist, and had the intellectual tools to wrestle with the spiritual questions of modernity and not simply brush them aside. For these reasons, his writings have offered guidance for the spiritually perplexed in our times.

It is of fundamental importance to understand that when Jung takes up and uses the religious language of his ancestors, he is using the terminology in a symbolic and a psychological sense rather than in a literal or metaphysical sense. He does not speak of God, for instance, as traditional religious people or theologians do, namely as a metaphysical and transcendent being, but rather of God images, which are generated by a psychological agency, the archetype. This is essential to keep in mind when reading Jung on religious themes and images. Much confusion has arisen and much ink spilled pointlessly as a result of misunderstanding his position on this critical point.

In an earlier work, *Jung's Treatment of Christianity*, I discussed the biographical and intellectual background and reasons for Jung's many writings on Christian doctrines and his extensive conversations and exchanges with its theological representatives. Briefly stated, I argued there that Jung in his mature years (roughly after the age of 60) took it upon himself to offer Christianity a type of psychotherapeutic treatment. This would be psychotherapy for culture, an extension of individual psychotherapy. Jung's treatment was directed at Christianity's deeply ingrained tendency to split the polarities of the human psyche into irreconcilable opposites: good against evil, masculine against feminine, spirit against body. In healthier philosophical and religious systems like Taoism, for instance, these polarities are seen as essentially related and existing in a dialectical and dynamic relation to one another. In Christianity, they are eternally warring opposites. As such, they foster neurotic conditions. Moreover, he saw that Christianity was becoming feeble as a religious and cultural force in the world and would be destined for extinction unless it found a way to heal these internal conflicts within its collective manifestation. He wanted to offer it a way out of this impasse. In the end, he recognized that he had failed in this project. The patient was not interested in pursuing wholeness.

Nevertheless, the effort left a trail of hints for a possible way forward in our own troubled times. This is a way, however, that will be distasteful to traditionalists and also unacceptable to many moderns. It is what I will call a third way, neither pre-modern/traditional nor modern/secular. It is a vision for a new type of humanism based on the idea of integration of the divine into the human, which amounts to the incarnation of the full *imago Dei* for all who accept the challenge. This is the challenge and the opportunity that psychology offers, a challenge to the traditional religious notion of a supernatural metaphysical God and an opportunity for a future in which spirituality will be woven into the fabric of conscious and everyday life. For this, however, a huge shift in thinking needs to take place that will transpose the theological Gods of traditional religions into psychological God-images available for integration into human consciousness.

This vision of a possible path to spirituality for modern people finds vigorous expression in Jung's late and highly controversial work, *Answer to Job*. There he states: "God wanted to become man, and still wants to" (Jung 1954: para. 739). The daunting implications of this idea remain to be worked out, and in what follows I will attempt to make a start. It has to do with individuation in the fullest sense of the word.

Answer to Job grew in part out of a long exchange with the Dominican professor of theology at Blackfriars, Oxford, Victor White, O.P. That dialogue marks a highpoint in Jung's attempt to engage creatively and therapeutically with Christianity. The relationship between the two men is richly detailed in their correspondence, begun in 1945 when Jung was 70 years old. The exchanges with White engaged him profoundly on several levels, but most especially with respect to the pressing problem of the relationship between analytical psychology and traditional Christian theology and practice. By entering into an intense emotional and intellectual relationship with Victor White, Jung gained further insight into the psychological conflicts that rage within the Christian psyche, particularly in a person who attempts to include the psychological attitude while trying to remain faithful to the Roman Catholic tradition of priesthood at the same time. His book, *Answer to Job*, published in German in 1952 and in English translation in 1954, appeared in the midst of their dialogue. In part it can be read as specifically addressed to White, but clearly it was also meant for all of Christendom. Its audience includes anyone who lives within and participates in a predominantly Christian culture. It is Jung's answer to the problems engendered within the Christianized psyche, and those who seek to remain faithful and committed to the Christian mythos do not easily digest it. For Victor White, the message of *Answer to Job* turned out to be too divergent from his religious and philosophical convictions and effectively ended the attempt at collaboration with Jung. In fact, White thought that Jung was betraying his own psychological theories by criticizing the God image of Christianity and venturing such strange ideas as a continuing incarnation and "the Christification of many" (Jung 1954, para. 758). Jung, he felt, was inviting archetypal inflation and paranoia.

What is the radical message that Jung is communicating in *Answer to Job*? Basically, it is the idea that the location of the biblical drama has shifted from the metaphysical and mythical to the psychological realm, and that human beings are themselves individually now responsible for redemption, atonement, and the reconciliation of the opposites, not a transcendent God "out there" in a supernatural realm. For the modern person, salvation and atonement come no longer from above, they must now come from within. The age of the psychological is upon us. This is a huge problem, but it is also a huge opportunity for further development of the human being.

In the West, and increasingly worldwide today in all modernizing societies, the cultural vanguard has left mythical and metaphysical thinking behind and has moved on to a secularist, pragmatic and instrumental attitude and a materialist philosophical outlook. The platform of consciousness attained by modernity is no longer subject to the authority of religious creeds or figures. It is secular, scientific, and increasingly individual. It is also averse to abstract metaphysical speculation. Valid and relevant knowledge must be grounded in research and experience, not based on faith or trust in religious authorities, whether texts or persons. This means that individuals have to re-imagine their purpose and destiny post-mythologically and post-metaphysically. They must look to a different source of inspiration and information to carry them forward since the logic of theo-logy no longer illuminates the human condition. A new kind of light must be turned on in the darkness of modernity if spirituality is to be found in contemporary terms. This would come, Jung surmised, from the logos of psyche, psycho-logy. But what is "psyche," and what is its logos? Certainly it is human, it is natural, and it is grounded in the body. But it also may observe and think deeply about hints of transcendence, as we shall see in later chapters.

Answer to Job is a psychological commentary on the Bible and the biblical tradition from the beginnings in ancient times to the present. As biblical interpretation, it does not belong or subscribe to any particular religious tradition or perspective, whether Hebrew or Christian, and it is equally unfettered by the conventions of modern historical inquiry and scholarship. It is neither religious nor academic; it is psychological. In Jung's hands, this meant that it would be governed by the rules of psychological dynamics, most importantly by the rules of individuation. That is to say, the psychological interpretation follows the logic of the psyche and its development (individuation), and it also importantly includes emotion and intuition within its methodology. The interpreter's psychological reactions to the text are essential to the hermeneutic, since the interpreter fully recognizes that there is a personal relationship with the text and works within this relationship. The interpreter's psyche is self-consciously at the center of the interpretation and therefore takes responsibility for the result. *Answer to Job* gives us a vivid taste of what psychological interpretation can produce in the hands of a master.

As Jung lays out his psychological perspective on the Book of Job and the rest of the Bible, he creates a unique and astonishing narrative of the biblical God-image's individuation. God is the main character of the Bible, and in this sense is a literary figure or, as Jung would say, a God-image, not the Godhead as it might be in and of itself. He creates a distance between the text and the referent. The arc of the biblical narrative runs from the creation of the world to the end of time and tells of the biblical God-image's psychological development. In *Answer to Job*, Jung himself achieves a supreme act of authorship, which in some ways surpasses that of Thomas Mann and even Goethe, both of whom took up the theme of God's wager with Satan in their respective works, *Doctor Faustus* and *Faust*. In effect, Jung rewrites the supreme fiction of Christendom, the Bible. In *Answer to Job*, we find what Harold Bloom refers to as a "strong misreading", which creates the possibility of a great poem. *Answer to Job* is a poem of the psyche that lays out a vision for a new kind of humanism, one that is not religious in any traditional sense of the word but is also not atheistic or secular. It is spiritual but shorn of all metaphysical assumptions. It advocates knowledge by experience, a type of modern gnosis.

Here is a summary of Jung's misreading, about which the theologian Karl Barth said correctly that it reflects the mind of the psychologist, not the mind of God.

Jung places the Book of Job at the center of the biblical narrative. This enigmatic book is the pivot point upon which the psychological transformation of the Bible's main character, the God image, Yahweh, turns. In the Book of Job, God is found guilty of unconsciousness and misconduct. God is utterly wrong in treating Job as He does. In the blameless and noble figure of Job, God confronts a level of consciousness superior to His own. Job holds his ground and shows supreme integrity, while God shows sheer unconsciousness and arrogant misuse of power. Human consciousness has outstripped the divine in the sense that Job is right in his pleas of innocence and God is in the wrong in treating him as His inferior. In the confrontation with Job, God has been found inept and cruel. He has violated his own sense of justice, broken his covenant, and lost his integrity. He has mobbed Job through the so-called comforters, and Job has become a scapegoat in his community. Yahweh is miserably out of contact with His own supreme Wisdom, Sophia, His feminine counterpart from eternity. After the rude episode with Job, God realizes that power cannot prevail over righteousness, and so he is forced to reconstitute Himself and make amends. First of all, He must recognize his inferiority to mankind. The critical issue is shadow awareness. God had not been fully aware of what he was doing. He had treated Job unjustly. First, he gave his left hand, Satan, the freedom to test the faithful but frail human's fidelity by stripping him bare of earthly possessions, family, and health, and then when Job had proven equal to the test and retained his integrity, God had reacted angrily with a display of might that overruled Job's plea for justice. Clearly, God had betrayed Job, first by mistreating him, a righteous man, and then by reducing him to impotent silence. God's vaunted wisdom and justice were totally absent in this display of frivolous mischief.

This drama produces a crisis in God's conscience. As a psychological factor, the God image can be influenced and affected by what is going on in consciousness. The God image, even though it is collective and embedded deeply within the archetypal layers of the unconscious, is not beyond the reach of consciousness but is actually powerfully affected by what transpires within the consciousness of the individual. In order to catch up with Job and regain His moral standing, God enters into a profound relationship with man and becomes incarnated as an individual person within His own creation. Thus an important aspect of the archetypal self actually enters into the domain of ego consciousness. Now God's experience of suffering, in and through the life of the human figure, Jesus of Nazareth, becomes equal in quality and degree to that which He had earlier inflicted upon Job. God's life as a human being culminates in an experience of betrayal and abandonment – the crucifixion. Like Job, Jesus became a scapegoat, first lifted up as an ideal and then violently rejected by the mob. When Jesus utters from the cross, "My God, my God, why hast Thou forsaken me?" God fully partakes in what Job experienced. Jesus had placed his trust in his Father in Heaven, and this trust is betrayed in a moment of total abandonment. God, as incarnated in Jesus, now suffers the same identical betrayal that Job had suffered by trusting in Him. This is God's heartfelt "answer to Job". The betrayer becomes the betrayed, and so experiences the full effect of His own shadow. The reversal is complete, and the result is greater consciousness. In this, God advances in consciousness and brings his own up to the standard set by Job. This represents an enormous increase in consciousness on the part of the archetypal self. It is a historic advance of consciousness on a collective level.

In fact, however, God surpasses Job because he recognizes his own infidelity, something Job never did or had to do. A God image is reborn from this ordeal as a figure of unimaginably higher standing than He held before, a model of integrated consciousness. This represents a dramatic change in the God image, from an arbitrary Power to a Being conscious of His own shadow and taking responsibility for it. This is a new God image and a psychologically advanced image of Divinity. In this, the archetypal self, which is the basis of all God images worldwide and in all mythologies and theologies, has achieved a new level of individuation.

In the biblical narrative, all of this takes place at the level of myth where God is seen as transcendent but undergoes a change from the characterization in the

Old Testament to that in the New Testament. At the psychological level, this development indicates a possibility for the God image to become more inclusive of "the opposites", good and evil, masculine and feminine, and to bring them into a better relationship with one another. Biblical religion had the chance to approach the Taoist vision of opposites in a dialectical relationship with one another. This would find expression in a universal and inclusive religion, which Christianity proposed in its early days but sadly did not realize as it succumbed to splitting tendencies active in the theological mind and in the cultural milieu of the ancient world.

Coming forward to the present time, human consciousness as we know it today in modern culture has advanced past, or out of, the pre-modern state of mythical and metaphysical consciousness. With this development comes the psychological attitude, a new way of thinking about religious experience and imagination. In this new paradigm, the psyche takes the place once occupied by the divine. The self, the central archetype of the collective unconscious, occupies the position of what was considered earlier a supernatural deity. We speak of God images, which are products of the archetypal self, rather than of metaphysical gods and goddesses. The human psyche has become the central player in the narrative, the subject and object of individuation processes at work consciously and unconsciously. The psyche is now seen as the locus of heavens and hells, of mythological beings like gods and goddesses, of angels and devils, and so forth. The psyche is now regarded as the source of their existence and as the ground upon which the conflicts that once raged in imagined supernatural realms and among its denizens is to be located. It is within the psyche that these noisy battles must be won, lost, or endured; and with this enormous shift in human consciousness comes the psychological and the ethical responsibility that human beings, individually and collectively, take up the challenge of individuation. What was once myth is now read as a psychological story, and the implications of this change in awareness are enormous for humanity.

For example, in traditional Christian theology, the myth of incarnation is generally regarded as a unique event in which God became man in the person of Jesus Christ. This happened only once and it will not, and cannot, happen again. Jung recasts the notion of incarnation in a psychological mode as a developmental process in which the unconscious becomes assimilated into consciousness over the period of an individual's lifetime. He calls this process individuation. For modern men and women, incarnation means entering actively and consciously into the individuation process, which requires enduring the battle of the opposites as they come into play and submitting to the extreme suffering of this conflict as Jesus Christ suffered on the cross, a symbol of hanging between the opposites. This suffering for the sake of individuation is for Jung the genuine *imitatio Christi*, which no longer means becoming Christ-like in the traditional sense of trying to become perfect as Christ was perfect or following his example. Rather, it means enduring the agony of the inner warring opposites until a unifying symbol is born in the individual soul. In other words, each person is required to incarnate the full complexity of the psyche, conscious and unconscious. This is what it means to "mind the self".

Individuals who take up the task of individuation must bear the suffering of the conflict of opposites inherent in their own nature. In this modern consciousness, people cannot dodge fundamental conflicts by embracing a comforting notion like, "God will take care of it." That would be to shrink from the essential task. The God image does not function apart from the human anymore. Atonement (at-one-ment) arrives from within through individual struggle to become conscious, not from without by divine intervention. Irrational and implacable suffering is meaningful if assumed consciously. To take this responsibility is now the human task. The shadow cannot any longer be swept under the carpet but must be taken on board consciously. The war between good and evil must be faced within each individual soul, and to suffer this conflict consciously is hugely meaningful for the individual and ultimately for the collective. This is Jung's deepest argument in *Answer to Job*.

According to this understanding of modernity, humans have now arrived at a type of consciousness that no longer subscribes to the literal meaning of myth and metaphysics. Bereft of comforting myths to live by, the modern person paradoxically stands where the biblical Job stood, and where Jesus hanging on the cross found himself – alone, abandoned, myths shattered, and evil starkly revealed. How can individuals cope with this horror? To return to myth and religious belief is impossible because modern consciousness has moved out of that mindset into a new territory, and there is no way back. The way forward must be psychological, which means that a new kind of conscious attitude must come into being that does not depend on the backing or comfort of a myth of transcendently given relief. There must be a different way. It is the psychological.

For the traditional Christian, the Church has offered protection from such anguishing dilemmas. The essential battle between good and evil has either already been won through the victory of Christ over Satan and by his resurrection, or it will be won by God in the end times when Satan will be defeated and locked away forever. The major opus of salvation is completed on the mythic level. The believer must only have faith that God has done (or will do) the job and get on board the collective vessel of the Church, passively accept the gift of grace, and cling to the assurance that all will be well.

What Jung announces in his *Answer to Job* is the bad news that this is not good enough any longer. Today everything decisive hangs on the balance of the human psyche. Will the individual human being endure the conflict and resolve the tension of the opposites, or will people choose to split the opposites and violently and unconsciously unleash the awesome powers delivered by science to destroy the earth? "Everything now depends on man: immense power of destruction is given into his hand, and the question is whether he can resist the will to use it, and can temper his will with the spirit of love and wisdom" (Jung 1954, para. 745). Jung's powerful sermonic poem invites people who are no longer secured in the big vessel of Church to get into their small individual boats and deal with the high seas on their own. But is the frail and vulnerable human individual capable of surviving the crushing waves of the warring opposites? This is the giant dilemma that faces humankind today. What can deliver us?

In the end, Jung discovered through his long and intense dialogue with Victor White that his vision for humanity and his understanding of the human condition were incompatible with Christian orthodoxy. His message could not be contained within the framework of this tradition. As he says in his last letter to White: "New wine needs new skins" (Lammers and Cunningham 2007: 287).

Chapter 2

Making room for divinity

Now I want to place further theoretical foundations under the notion of incarnation for all, which Jung expressed poetically and so forcefully in his *Answer to Job*. This is meant to answer the question: What are we as human beings to do? The answer to this is related to the meaning of individuation, the development of the human potential in us from our origin in the womb to its completion in the course of a lifetime of experience and reflection. We are meant to individuate. Psychological theory must provide the new wineskin for the new wine that is being pressed out by modern experience. What else do we have? Psychological theory can be a container and can orient our thinking, as theology and mythology did in earlier ages. It can help us to integrate into our identity and worldview the new and unusual or surprising insights that arise directly from personal experience. Most importantly, it gives us a way to perceive the meaning of our labors in individuation.

The centerpiece in this psychological theory rests in the meaning of what Jung called the self. It is generally recognized by anyone even a little familiar with Jung's writings that he drew a critically important distinction between the meaning of the terms ego and self. On this point he was exceptionally clear and consistent. The term self refers to a hypothetical psychic domain that encompasses all aspects of the ego complex and the surrounding penumbra of actual and potential consciousness. It includes conscious and unconscious aspects of the ego complex, including its defenses, as well as forgotten or momentarily absent psychic contents that could be brought up into consciousness with some effort or assistance. Moreover, the self surpasses even this large complex of psychic material in several respects: its range and scope of reference is far greater in extension, in that it subsumes all conscious and unconscious levels and aspects of the psyche under its aegis. In theoretical range, it is therefore also more complex, because it embraces all the polarities and tensions within the psyche as a whole and not only those within consciousness and the ego complex; and it transcends the conscious/unconscious divide. The self is responsible for the underlying unity of the psyche as a whole, whereas the ego complex provides some measure of unity only for consciousness. The relation of the terms ego and self is that of a part to the whole.

With the notion of self, therefore, Jung was postulating a psychological dimension that far exceeds the limits of individuals' usual conscious self-awareness, identity, sense of self, and experience of psychic reality. Most importantly, it provides a key to the modern person to open the door to transcendence and spirituality and a link to traditional religious forms of spirituality. This is because the self, as the central archetype of the collective unconscious, is the source of all archetypal images, including God-images, which are to be found in the world's religions and mythologies. The self hypothesis, therefore, stretches our thinking about the human psyche beyond the secular range of self-knowledge toward the unknown-within, toward the mystery of existence, toward a personal relation to and possible inclusion in the infinite, and toward the numinous and the holy (Rudolf Otto 1917/1950).

Within the limits of the ego complex, we are focused, defined, defended, and somewhat cognizant of our thoughts, feelings, and the grounds for our emotional conditions; we have a personal and social identity more or less unified and singular, a sense of self that is bounded and unique. As the self, on the contrary, we are utterly indeterminate, infinitely extended, never fully realized, and linked to (even fused with) the transcendent source and ground of being. The self grounds the ego complex in ultimate wholeness. It encompasses all the psyche's inherent inner oppositions and obscurities, the shadows, and the numerous contradictions and riddles one has to live with in respect to an ever-shifting focus of ego identity and identification. Self arches high up above the chasms that cut through the personality, linking and containing the persona and the shadow (good and bad), the gendered ego complex and the anima/animus (masculine and feminine), and conscious and unconscious. Self is what we are above, beneath, and beyond all identities, identifications, and part-personalities – personal, cultural, historical, engendered, and moral. It is what we are when all that we know or suspect that we are is added together, *plus* what we are when all that is stripped away. It is the source of psychic life and therefore the bottomless reservoir of religious experience.

Jung studied the mystery of the self continuously in the later decades of his life. I am following some hints from his late works in proposing an ontological ground for the self, for the question naturally arises: What is the source and origin of the self? As the ego is nested in the self, so the self is nested in a still wider ontological ground. Here we touch on the truly transcendent and reach beyond the psychic realm of the individual to the cosmic ground of Being. However, this is not a return to the mythological, which would be a regression to an earlier age and stage of consciousness.

Jung's *Mysterium Coniunctionis* is a late literary and theoretical work on the self. As the title suggests, the book is concerned especially with uniting the polarities inherent in the self and with the prospect for overcoming the psyche's chief divide, that between conscious and the unconscious. At the outset, Jung flatly announces "the polaristic structure of the psyche" as a given (Jung 1955/1963: xvi). The opus of alchemy was to unite the opposites, Jung declares, and so is the goal of analysis. From here on, however, his way forward in this work is anything but direct. *Mysterium Coniunctionis* is, like the psyche itself, replete with ambiguities, and for the translator it must have been a full-blown nightmare.

The passage that I will lift from this work for close inspection here occurs in the chapter titled "Luna", in a sub-section called "The Dog". Jung writes: "Kalid's 'son of the dog' is the same as the much extolled 'son of the philosophers'. The ambiguity of this figure is thus stressed: it is at once bright as day and dark as night, a perfect *coincidentia oppositorum*...". (Jung 1955/1963: para.176). "Son of the Philosophers" is for Jung an alchemical synonym of the self. Because "Kalid's son of the dog" designates the "son of the philosophers", the ambiguous nature of self is emphasized here to an extraordinary degree. For the Arab author, "son of the dog" would be a curse; on the other hand, "Son of the Philosophers" is the most elevated accolade. Hence Jung's comment: the self is "at once bright as day and dark as night", a perfect coincidence of opposites. The tension could not be greater.

Completing the sentence, we find Jung writing this treacherous German phrase: "*als welche die Göttlichkeit das Selbst ausdrückt.*" R.F.C. Hull, translator of the *Collected Works*, renders this as: "expressing the divine nature of the self" (Jung 1955/1963: para. 176). The sentence thus reads in English: "...it is at once bright as day and dark as night, a perfect *coincidentia oppositorum* expressing the divine nature of the self." This is not an accurate translation, however, but rather more of a personal interpretation, or maybe even an error. Literally translated, the text would read (very awkwardly!): "... a perfect *coincidentia oppositorum*, as how the Divinity expresses the self." Jung is clearly not saying here that the self has a divine nature, as Hull's translation would have it, but rather that "Divinity" (*die Göttlichkeit*) expresses or shapes or molds (*ausdrückt*) the self, in the form of a *coincidentia oppositorum*. It is a kind of restatement of the idea of the human being as shaped in the image of God (*imago Dei*). As Jung announced at the beginning of *Mysterium Coniunctionis*, the psyche is structured as a polarity. Now he tells us what is responsible for this structure. It is attributed to *die Göttlichkeit*. In the original German, there is a clear distinction between *die Göttlichkeit* and the self, and nothing is said about the self's nature, only about its structure as a "coincidence of opposites". This structure is given by *die Göttlichkeit*.

The term *die Göttlichkeit* does not translate easily into English. It is a noun made from an adjective: *göttlich* = divine-like, like a Deity, made of a divine substance. *Die Göttlichkeit* is, moreover, not a specific Deity. Jung is not repeating the Biblical story of Adam's and Eve's creation by Yahweh in his own image in the Garden of Eden. As a noun, the attribute is made into a substance, as when we go in English from the adjective "high" to the noun "Highness", as in "His Highness". *Die Göttlichkeit* (I will translate it as Divinity) is not definite, and so is unlike such specific deities as Osiris, Apollo, Yahweh, Wotan, and so forth. Divinity is the quality they all share in common, here raised to the level of an essence. It is this essence that makes them divine and distinguishes them from things non-divine. It is this archetypal essence that gives the God and Goddess figures the quality of Deity, otherwise they would appear as just slightly larger than life-size figures, like heroes. *Die Göttlichkeit* is Jung's way of referring to what Paul Tillich calls the Absolute itself, which is Being-Itself, and beyond the specific deities of the religions (Tillich 1967: 127).

To repeat, Jung is not *equating* the self with Divinity or saying that the self is divine, as some of his interpreters and critics have claimed. He is saying that Divinity forms and shapes the self into a pattern that manifests as an internal polarity. The Divinity and the self thus mirror one another. In this way, the self reflects the Ground of Being and is therefore intimately related to the universe. Humanity belongs essentially to the cosmos not by virtue of common material elements, but because at bottom the psyche is reflective of the deepest ontological structures, of Being itself. The psyche is linked, in short, to a transcendent factor called Divinity that shapes it structurally.

Divinity is the ontological ground of the self as it takes shape in individuals' psychic structures and of all instances of the self in human beings generally. All human beings are linked to the same ontological Ground, and each is fundamentally structured according to the architecture of this ontological Ground. However, the relationship between the self and Divinity, its ontological Ground, is incommensurate, in that the former is an instantiation of the latter but by no means a complete one. An individual can strive to individuate as far as is possible, and in this sense incarnate the self, but no single person can incarnate the Ground of Being completely because it far exceeds the capacities of an individual self. Some humans may approach a state of full incarnation of the self, but none, even the great spiritual figures of history like Buddha and Christ, have achieved full incarnation of the Ground of Being despite theological claims to the contrary. All are limited by their times and their cultures. These images of selfhood are only partial representations of the full self and always leave some important elements of the self out of their portraits. Besides, their mythical stature is the product of archetypal projections from others and so not truly reflective of their individual attainments. However, such figures suggest what can be accomplished in the course of the individuation process and offer us models for incarnation of Divinity within the possibilities of the self as given to the individual at a particular moment in history and within a specific cultural context.

Traditional deities in the world's great and small religions have been the product of projections of archetypal psychological forces that reflect potential images inherent in the self. These archetypal images of the psyche are living and dynamic powers, as Jung stresses in many passages. The ultimate God-image of the monotheistic religions expresses the archetype of the self as the "central archetype of order". The gods and goddesses of the polytheistic religions express facets of the self, reflecting the anima/animus levels of the psyche. None of these, however, are full expressions of the Ground of Being, Divinity itself. They are humanly generated images based upon emotionally convincing numinous experiences and the mythopoetic and theological imagination. The religions claim for their assertions the authority of revelation, but modernity discounts the ultimacy of this claim and psychology regards its contents as projection.

The self is an *imago Dei*, in Jung's account, in the sense that it conforms to the architecture inherent in the Ground of Being. This is a hypothesis, a theory. Since epistemology limits human knowledge of what can be known to the parameters of the human mind and does not allow us to step out of the psyche and know things as they are in themselves (Kant's *Ding an sich*, which is the same as Jung's archetype *per se*), when we imagine ultimate reality (the Ground of Being itself) and project this image into the unknown that is named Divinity, we find only what we can know of the self and not the self archetype *per se*. It is a theoretical move to assert that the self we know, an archetypal image, accurately reflects the self *per se*, or the Divinity. Otherwise we would again be saying that our God-image is final and reflects Divinity accurately and perfectly. At best, we can know the Ground of Being only indirectly by what it offers for incarnation in the form of new images, intuitions, and visions. Incarnation of the self is evolutionary and open-ended. The human psyche is the window through which the Divinity may enter into consciousness, however partially or fully.

Some of his detractors have accused Jung of coming too close to claiming knowledge of the ultimate Ground of Being, as though he were a Gnostic prophet pretending to possess insider information about Divinity itself. In a fierce debate with Martin Buber, who had characterized Jung as a modern Gnostic and in fact named him as a secret devotee of Abraxas, a Gnostic God figure who is mentioned in Jung's *Red Book* and in the visionary "*Septem Sermones ad Mortuos*", Jung became somewhat ironic but also self-revealing:

> Here, just for once, and as an exception, I shall indulge in transcendental speculation and even in 'poetry': God has indeed made an inconceivably sublime and mysteriously contradictory image of himself, without the

help of man, and implanted it in man's unconscious as an archetype, an ἀρχέτυπον φῶς, archetypal light: not in order that theologians of all times and places should be at one another's throats, but in order that the unpresumptuous man might glimpse an image, in the stillness of his soul, that is akin to him and is wrought of his own psychic substance. This image contains everything he will ever imagine concerning his gods or concerning the ground of his psyche.

(Jung 1952/1976: para. 1508)

While Jung says this ostensibly with tongue in cheek, the idea here is nearly identical to the one expressed in *Mysterium Coniunctionis*, which was written at about the same time and contains in the phrase: "*als welche die Göttlichkeit das Selbst ausdrückt.*" In both instances, *die Göttlichkeit* (Divinity) implants the self (named an ἀρχέτυπον φῶς in the reply to Buber) within the human being as a psychological fundament. This is the self archetype *per se*. Inscribed in the psyche as an archetype, the self is the source and the point of origin of all humanly elaborated mythologies and theologies, none of which is or can be a complete or wholly accurate description of Divinity itself. The world's religions and mythologies can be read for the information that they provide about the human psyche in which they are grounded and which they reflect, but they should not be absolutized and ontologized. They are images that reflect the archetypal unconscious. They can be regarded as only relatively accurate statements about the psyche in its archetypal depths; they do not, however, define or exhaustively describe the ontological ground of the psyche. The self *per se*, as distinguished from the many self images and as the fundamental psychic ground of all images and ideas of Divinity, is thus grounded in and fused with a deeper ontological ground. From the structure of the self, one can possibly infer that the Ground of Being is also a *unio oppositorum* (otherwise why would the self be such?), but that is the limit of human knowledge concerning Divinity. The rest is projection and sheer speculation based on human assumptions and psychological dynamics.

The human task is to incarnate as much of the self, and therefore also of what stands behind the self, which is the Ground of Being, as possible in a single lifetime. This is the task of individuation, and it is what I mean by minding the self. The task of humanity as a whole is to incarnate the Ground of Being as fully as possible on a collective level. This has been the project of the world's religions until modern times, for better or worse. Since the onset of modernity, however, more fully conscious individuals must take this up. The traditional religions are tied up in their metaphysical intuitions and thus limited in scope. They are not open to new revelations of the self. Perhaps in time individuals can build a structure for a future collective expression of a more complete rendition of the Ground of Being on a collective level, an incarnation of the

Divinity on a worldwide collective level. This is a task for the ages and one that can be measured only in aeons, long spans of time like the Platonic Years, which occupy two thousand calendar years apiece. However, with the acceleration so evident in the contemporary world, these vast time periods may be hastened, and what would have taken thousands of years to accomplish earlier could be done now in shorter spaces of time. So far, however, there is scant evidence for this speed-up. Spirituality has certainly not kept up with the pace of technology and scientific discovery.

The practical question remains of how the infinitesimally small human individual, being limited to a singular consciousness with unconscious cultural blinders fixed in place besides, can possibly take account of a psychological universe that is so much greater than the ego. How do we, or can we, experience the self and integrate it more fully into our conscious life? We tend to build ghettoes for our conscious egos and lock ourselves in at night to avoid the troubling sounds from the lunar world of dreams. This ghettoization of the ego must be overcome and the defenses dismantled. Beyond that, can people incarnate the potentials inherent in the self and also let flashes and hints from the transcendent Divinity into their limited and so much narrower conscious horizon and integrate all this into their conscious attitudes and worldviews? This is the psychological challenge for the contemporary person. It is a question of increasing consciousness and opening the mind to its own unconscious background and beyond that to the soul of the world. This brings with it the shock of new or other God-images coming into view and upsetting some of our most precious assumptions about what is real and true.

Chapter 3

Changing and emerging God-images

Evidence that old God-images can and do change over time and that new ones emerge has been widely available since the advent of modern historical consciousness. The detailed scholarly reconstruction of the past that took hold in the eighteenth and nineteenth centuries had the effect of undermining the sense that religious objects remain permanently fixed. Some scholars saw the changes as bad and a sign of decay or deterioration from a former purity (Adolph Harnack, for instance, who commented critically on the Hellenization of Christian theology in the early centuries of the Common Era). Others regarded them as evolutionary and a sign of development and maturation (Cardinal John Henry Newman, for example). Still other thinkers found this as proof positive that God-images are illusions that are bent to the service of ulterior motives of one kind or another (Feuerbach, Marx, Nietzsche, Freud). In recent decades, the interest in including feminine images of the Godhead of Christian theology has become urgent.

Questions regarding why such changes take place and what they mean can cause grave disorientation and anxiety. If as seemingly permanent a cultural object as a God-image is subject to change and mutation, what is stable anymore? Is there no fixed and stable foundation that people can rely on? No "Rock of Ages"? Is everything in flux? Uncertainties abound. Moderns were made anxious by this state of affairs; post-moderns have tended to celebrate it. Fundamentalists, of course, ignore the issue altogether and cling to traditional certainties.

If one casts an unprejudiced eye across cultures and over long time periods, it is obvious that God-images can be found in an enormous variety of manifestations. Even a brief survey of world religions will yield a list of scores of them. A God-image appears whenever people attempt to describe a numinous experience and give formal definition to the *mysterium tremendum*. The image derives from imagination, the unseen being placed into a visible container, be it as animal, plant, human, or abstract form. The cluster of attributes ascribed to this invisible presence, made at least partially visible or articulated in language, defines the God image further. The biblical God figure, for example, who forbids images and demands to remain invisible and therefore transcendent, does receive verbal definition in the texts of revelation and with such verbalized attributes as Shepherd, Father, Creator, Sustainer, Judge and so forth.

Many of the God-images found among world religions have features similar to others, while differing in detail and nuance depending on the social and theological context in which they are embedded. For instance, there are Father Gods and Mother Goddesses, Savior Gods, Sky Gods and Goddesses, Earth and Underworld Deities. Categorization of them is possible and instructive.

In addition to the God-images based and rooted in religious and cultural traditions, there are still others to be found in the accounts of individuals, and often these are based on dreams and visions and supplemented by reflective commentaries. These may have qualities similar to those that are enshrined by cultures, and most of them can be similarly typed and categorized.

In Jungian terms, a God-image is a partial representation of the self, not of the ego or the personal complexes. This is the difference from Freudian interpretations of God-images as representations of the parental complexes. A God-image is a numinous symbol derived from the archetypal level of the psyche, which captures and conveys an intuition or feeling of awe-inspiring, absolute, cosmic, eternal Being. Such symbols can lead us directly to an experience of the archetypal world. As symbols, these images communicate and mediate a dimension of Being that lies beyond the ego's limitations, beyond the confines of humanly-perceivable boundaries of time and space.

Here are two striking examples of a God-image. The first is a literary one from the Bible, and the second is from an orally-reported dream of a contemporary woman. First, the classic one from the Bible:

> After this I looked, and lo, in heaven an open door …. At once I was in the spirit, and lo, a throne stood in heaven, with one seated on the throne! And he who sat there appeared like jasper and carnelian, and round the throne was a rainbow that looked like an emerald. Round the throne were twenty-four thrones, and seated on the thrones were twenty-four elders, clad in white garments, with golden crowns upon their heads. From the throne issue flashes of lightening, and voices and peals of thunder, and before the throne burn seven torches of fire, which are the seven spirits of God; and before the throne there is as it were a sea of glass, like crystal.
>
> And round the throne, on each side of the throne, are four living creatures, full of eyes in front and behind; the first living creature like a lion, the second living creature like an ox, the third living creature with a face like a human face, and the fourth living creature like a flying eagle. And the

four living creatures, each of them with six wings, are full of eyes round and within, and day and night they never cease to sing,

"Holy, holy, holy, is the Lord God Almighty,
who was and is and is to come!"

… And between the throne and the four living creatures and among the elders, I saw a Lamb standing, as though it had been slain, with seven horns and with seven eyes, which are the seven spirits of God sent out into all the earth; and he went and took the scroll from the right hand of him who was seated on the throne. When he had taken the scroll, the four living creatures and the twenty-four elders fell before the Lamb, each holding a harp, and with golden bowls full of incense, which are the prayers of the saints…
… And I heard every living creature in heaven and on earth and under the earth and in the sea, and all that therein, saying, "To him who sits upon the throne and to the Lamb be blessing and honor and glory and might for ever and ever!" And the four living creatures said, "Amen!" and the elders fell down and worshiped.

(Revelations 4:1–5:14, RSV)

In this magnificent example of a traditional God-image, one recognizes the essential features of a God-image: a) numinosity (awesome power, wonder, and fear on the part of the human observer); b) absolute ontological standing, and c) cosmic proportion. In The Book of Revelation, we read that this image came to the author in a vision. In the literary account of this vision, one recognizes quotations from earlier biblical passages. This does not disqualify it as a genuine vision, that is, a spontaneous manifestation of an unconscious archetype. The recipient of the vision was obviously steeped in the Bible, and his unconscious also contained these contents. In the vision, the more familiar, learned images are combined with other newly emergent archetypal images, and together they are presented as a new "revelation". This is a new God-image, albeit based on an older one. This illustrates how God-images evolve and change over time.

Moreover, this vision's symbolic nature is evident not because it contains familiar biblical images such as the four living creatures (a direct allusion to Ezekiel's vision), but because it goes beyond them and peers directly into the very heart of the *mysterium tremendum*. A God-image is a symbol that attempts to capture and make visible all that it can of the noumenal (i.e., the essentially hidden and irrepresentable) archetype *per se*, of Divinity itself. In this vision, recorded according to tradition by St John on the island of Patmos, we witness an awesome symbol of the self-archetype as presented to an individual human being's consciousness some two thousand years ago.

Jumping over two millennia to the present, here is a second example of a God-image, quite different from the first in several respects but comparable in symbolic value as a representation of the self. This is from the dream of a woman in her early sixties, a person not at all religious in a traditional or even a non-traditional New Age sense, but frequently gifted in her dreams with archetypal images of the collective unconscious. She is therefore what I would think of as a spiritual rather than a religious person.

I find myself in a large throng of people who are milling around, moving slowly. Suddenly I feel the ground beneath our feet shaking violently. A powerful charge of energy is moving up through the earth. I feel this powerful energy and now see that it has a form and moves among us in a figure eight on its side. Then I see that it is an enormous snake.

The snake's beautiful face appears to me. It has the head of a woman. The enormous body of the snake is covered with white orchids that are growing out of her.

She confronts me. Her giant face comes near, her dark eyes fix me in a stare, and of course I am afraid. Beyond the fear, though, I feel tremendous awe and wonder at this marvelous and remarkable being.

"Who are you?" she demands of me. "What do you do?" I give my name and tell her that I am a psychotherapist.

"Oh, so you are an architect of souls," she replies. I am surprised at this designation and listen further.

"You are like Julius Caesar and ...." (She names some other historical characters whom I cannot recall after I awaken). She must see the look of astonishment on my face because she goes on to say: "Of course you could not know that. Julius Caesar was an architect of souls in a much earlier time."

I now understand intuitively that this snake has been around since the beginning of time. Her memory holds a record of all the souls who have ever lived, and of all of their various incarnations and specific identities. Some souls have lived more than once, or even many times. I am surprised that she has placed me in a category with Julius Caesar and even more astonished that his underlying identity was an "architect of souls". Clearly I do not understand something important here. I am dumbfounded and shaken to be meeting a consciousness that has been around since the universe began.

For a time we simply look at each other. I admire the beautiful white orchids that cover her massive body. I also realize that she is immensely powerful and could annihilate me in an instant. But I decide to take a risk anyway and venture to say: "You now have an opportunity to do great good, because you are at a point in your evolution where you are on the

way to becoming fully conscious. You are more than halfway there."
Surprised at my own boldness, I wonder how she will take this comment.
   She smiles enigmatically. I take this as a blessing. Great streams of
energy are flowing from her.

Like the classic God-image from the Book of Revelation, the giant snake
image in this dream is a numinous symbol of the Divinity, in an animal and
feminine form, portraying a being of vast power and cosmic trans-temporal
dimension. Unlike the biblical God-image, however, this one emerges from
the earth and is not located high up in the heavens. The dream also remarkably
includes the notion of an evolving consciousness in the image of Divinity.
The snake Goddess, if I may call her such, does not claim the quality of
absolute omniscience and transcendence typical of the monotheistic Deity,
although she does show memory of all that has happened to date in human
and perhaps in cosmic history. Her consciousness is in process, now more
than halfway to completion, according to the dream speaker's assessment.
The claim made for the God-image of the monotheisms has been adamantly
that the God-image named and worshipped is omniscient and omnipotent,
anything but a work in progress. This other, new Goddess-image, on the
contrary, implies development within the Divinity's consciousness. History
and the passage of time make a difference at the archetypal level, according
to the dream. Moreover, the relation between the human observer and the
observed God-image is also very different in the two narratives. The second
is much more dialogical. One can hardly imagine St John conversing with the
One seated on the throne or with the Lamb, never mind commenting on their
degree of completeness or partiality in any manner whatsoever. While it is
certainly not correct to say that the dreamer's consciousness and that of the
serpent Goddess-image are on a par or depicted in any sense as equal, the words
of this dreamer are bold and even show a kind of superiority in that she can
pass judgment on the attainments to date of the Divinity.
   One might hazard the hypothesis that ego-consciousness has gained
considerable standing vis-à-vis the archetypal self in the last two thousand
years. This same increased standing of the ego in relation to a God-image is
represented in Jung's *Answer to Job*, where in a number of famous passages
Jung takes Yahweh to task for his lack of consciousness.
   A God-image, then, is a psychic image that captures an important aspect of
the self. Presented to the conscious ego, a God-image offers the benefit of a
symbol, which mediates between the ego and the archetypal self. The connecting link between the ego and the self – the so-called ego-self axis – is basically
made up God-images. This is as critically important to recognize for the
psychology of religion as it is for the psychotherapy of individuals. People need
and use God-images to establish a relationship to the self. Activities like prayer

and contemplation in religious life have a profound psychological value. Jung's use of active imagination functions as the equivalent to prayer in traditional contexts. This explains why people are so attached to their God-images and why they are so loath to give them up. Without a connection to the self, a person experiences emptiness, disorientation, and dread – the psychological pathos of modernity.

Chapter 4

The way of symbols

My personal physician once complained to me bitterly about the many patients he sees who are perfectly healthy but come to him doubled up in pain and complaining about their symptoms. "They are crazy", he said, throwing up his hands in frustration. "Perfectly healthy people, but not able to live with their health! On the other hand, I have patients who feel as healthy as can be, and I have to tell them they have six months to live because of a recently-discovered lymphoma. I'd like to send the healthy ones to the moon! They're nuts!"

His complaint reminded me of the opening pages of Jung's Terry Lectures at Yale University, *Psychology and Religion* (Jung 1936/1969). He is telling his audience about the power of neurosis over patients' lives. A man imagines he has cancer, for instance, he says, but there is no physical evidence for cancer in his body. Now he becomes convinced that he is crazy and so he consults Jung, the psychiatrist. "Help me, doctor. I'm dying from thinking nonsense, but I can't help it!" What does Jung do with this imaginary cancer?

> I told him that it would be better to take his obsession seriously instead of reviling it as pathological nonsense. But to take it seriously would mean acknowledging it as a sort of diagnostic statement of the fact that, in a psyche that really existed, trouble had arisen in the form of a cancerous growth. "But", he will surely ask, "what could that growth be?" And I shall answer: "I do not know", as indeed I do not. Although… it is surely a compensatory or complementary unconscious formation, nothing is yet known about its specific nature or about its content. It is a spontaneous manifestation of the unconscious, based on contents which are not to be found in consciousness… I then inform him… that his dreams will provide us with all the necessary information. We will take them as if they issued from an intelligent, purposive, and, as it were, personal source…. The symptom is like the shoot above ground, yet the main plant is an extended rhizome underground. The rhizome represents the content of a

neurosis; it is the matrix of complexes, of symptoms, and of dreams. We have every reason to believe that dreams mirror exactly the underground processes of the psyche. And if we get there, we literally get at the "roots" of the disease.

(Jung 1936/1969, paras. 35–37)

The point here is that the psychic symptom, in this case the delusional idea of a cancerous growth in a healthy body, is a symbol and as such can offer a point of contact with unconscious complexes, processes, unresolved conflicts, and even archetypal images. Like a physical cancer, if left unchecked, will suck the life out of a living organism, so a psychic cancer may well drain a person's life of psychic energy and produce a state of hopeless stagnation and neurotic misery. On the other hand, it may conceal an image of Divinity in disguise whose presence could herald an important change of consciousness. Symbols can be the means for incarnation of greater wholeness. They are the link to the self.

Symbols may resemble metaphors, even though they surpass them in depth and spiritual significance. In one sense, the symptom-as-symbol looks like a metaphor, in that it is borrowing the language of physicality (cancer, illness) and using it to indicate psychic illness (neurosis). This linguistic transfer from one domain to another is what poets do when they employ metaphors, so the psyche in this case is acting in a sort of poetic fashion by saying with conviction, "I am sick with cancer" when it should be saying, were it more literal and less poetic, "I am in despair", or "my libidinal sources are dying, I have no energy", or "I am in hopeless conflict and it's eating me alive!" But this patient cannot say that. He can only say, "I am convinced that I have cancer and I can't get this irrational idea out of my head!" He is an unwilling poet and has not chosen this metaphor consciously or voluntarily. It has chosen him, and he is helpless to dismiss it and unable to interpret it.

However, symbols should be seen as related to but different from metaphors. Metaphors remain within the domain of the rational and understandable, even if their application seems strained. If a poet says about a bridge that it "leaps" and that it is an "altar" and a "harp", as the American poet Hart Crane does about Brooklyn Bridge in his famous poem with that title, the reader can make out what he means to communicate with these images. If we know what the Brooklyn Bridge looks like, we can readily understand that ingenious images like "leaps", "altars" and "harps" apply poetically to the magnificent bridge and communicate the poet's vision and feeling. We can see and think along with the poet and appreciate his precise imagery and ingenious mastery of metaphor. But if someone says, "I am convinced that I have a cancerous tumour in my body but there is no evidence, what does this mean?" we must confess, with Jung, that the mistaken but obsessive idea does not have a clear meaning. It symbolizes something essentially unknown and perhaps unknowable, at least for the time being, even if it may well suggest a line of thought for possible elucidation. A precise understanding, however, depends upon many other variables, which are mostly hidden from the consciousness of the speaker and the hearer. A full interpretation requires deeper elucidation than is called for by a simple metaphor. Jung defines the symbol as follows:

> … the best possible formulation of a relatively *unknown* thing, which for that reason cannot be more clearly or characteristically represented …. So long as a symbol is a living thing, it is an expression for something that cannot be characterized in any other or better way. The symbol is alive only so long as it is pregnant with meaning. But once its meaning has been born out of it, once that expression is found which formulates the thing sought, expected, or divined even better than the hitherto accepted symbol, then the symbol is *dead*, i.e., it possess only an historical signifi-cance… An expression that stands for a known thing remains a mere sign and is never a symbol.
>
> (Jung 1921/1971: pars. 815–817)

In another text, he offers the following succinct definition of the symbol: "The symbol is not a sign that disguises something generally known – a disguise, that is, for the basic drive or elementary intention. Its meaning resides in the fact that it is an attempt to elucidate, by a more or less apt analogy, something that is still entirely unknown or still in the process of formation" (Jung 1928/1966, para. 492). So the symbol is a kind of vague analogy to something otherwise completely in the dark, unknown, and unconscious but obviously at the same time extremely psychologically important.

At the moment, the patient with the delusional idea of having a cancerous growth in his body cannot express his malady in any other or better way, or in a more accurate and precisely descriptive way. He is therefore speaking symbolically but has absolutely no conscious understanding of what the symbol of cancer means for him. For him, it is simply a delusional idea, a crazy thought that he can't shake. The thought is itself like a cancer in that it plagues him and grows uncontrollably. Nor does the doctor know precisely what it means. Does it conceal a big and growing unthinkable thought? A fear, like the fear of death? A death wish, because he cannot free himself from an untenable situation? A numinous presence that is haunting him? With symbols one knows only that they are trying to express something by anal-ogy, similar to a metaphor, but for the moment that is all. One is lacking the reference ("A" means "?"). Once the symbolic symptom is understood – be it as the outcome of a childhood trauma, be it as the outgrowth of intrapsychic or interpersonal conflict, be it as unexpressed and blocked creative potential, or whatever else the meaning may turn out to be – it can be put aside as a symbol and used thereafter as a metaphor or a kind of historical marker: "I used to think I had cancer, but what I found out was that my libido was blocked because of trauma, childhood conflicts, and consequent lack of self-confidence (or whatever) and that my psychic life was completely out of control." Once the necessary psychic meaning has been discovered and made conscious, the symbol becomes a sign ("A" means "B") and can then be used as a metaphor by consciousness if the patient chooses to be poetic. The referent is clear. The purpose of analysis is to convert symbols into signs and metaphors and so to free the patient's consciousness from the grip of the unconscious complexes and to unblock the flow of libido into more satisfying channels of living, loving, and creating. This opens the way for fuller incarnation of the self in a person's life.

It is generally much more important, however, to experience a symbol fully than to interpret it. Interpretation can be helpful for rational understanding, but it can also abort the birth of the symbol into consciousness and drain it of its energy and possibilities for further meaning. The symbol touches deep emotional levels that can lead to gradual integration in time. Sometimes symbols are never interpreted at all but carried in memory for years, perhaps gradually yielding to intellectual insight. At other times, the intellectual meaning is trivial beside the huge emotional impact of the symbol. For incarnational purposes it is essential to realize that:

> ... symbols act as *transformers*, their function being to convert libido from a 'lower' into a 'higher' form. This function is so important that feeling accords it the highest values. The symbol works by suggestion; that is to say, it carries conviction and at the same time expresses the content of that conviction. It is able to do this because of the numen, the specific energy stored up in the archetype. Experience of the archetype is not only impressive, it seizes and possesses the whole personality... the prime task of the psychotherapist must be to understand the symbols anew, and thus to understand the unconscious, compensatory striving of his patient for an attitude that reflects the totality of the psyche.
>
> (Jung 1912/1970: pars. 344–346)

Symbols have the capacity to sublimate psychic content and energy, transforming the unconscious factors at play into new forms, patterns, and preoccupations, thus sending energy into channels that tend toward "higher" i.e., more complex, motivations, activities, attitudes, and states of consciousness. Symbols are thus the agents of incarnation.

Symbols appear in many situations in life and most importantly and frequently in the dreaming state, to what I call the lunar mind in the following chapter.

The lunar mind is less rational than the waking solar mind and so is less constrained by the fences of acculturation. The lunar mind is not as ghettoized as the solar mind. In our dreams, we range far more widely afield in the psyche and more freely in the wide dimensions of the self than we do in waking life. Symbolic images emerge in our lives especially at critical developmental periods like adolescence, midlife, retirement and during times of personal crisis. Especially then is it useful to attend to dreams and to develop a capacity for living a symbolic life in the psychological sense.

A symbol is an intermediate stage of incarnation, halfway between sheer unconsciousness and conscious integration. The content embedded in the symbol is moving from the depths of the core self at the archetypal level toward the ego, and in this stage of emergence presents as an image or story that needs further energy to be made fully available to consciousness for purposes of individuation. Interpretation is often needed to assist in this movement toward conscious apprehension but can also be misleading or destructive. A bad interpretation can damage the soul by distorting or misreading the psychic content seeking to make its way into consciousness. As Jung writes in his brilliant and moving essay, "The psychology of the child archetype": "...whatever explanation or interpretation does to it, we do to our own souls as well, with corresponding results for our own well-being" (Jung 1940/1969: par. 27).

Chapter 5

Attending the lunar mind

We want to push further into the consideration of how one actually goes about minding the self. This is a huge psychological opus and takes an entire life-time to complete. Typically, individuation, or the incarnation of the self, takes place in life through two major movements, separation and integration. I have described these more fully in *The Principle of Individuation* (Stein 2006). Both separation and integration take place continuously and on many levels throughout a person's lifetime. The child separates from the mother in early years, later from the family of origin as well, and goes on to live a separate and independent life as an adult individual. Meanwhile, we find that on the inner level an ego grows out of the darkness of the unconscious psyche and gradually separates from its background, thereby creating a division between ego-consciousness and the unconscious. At later stages of psychological development, the individual separates from social and cultural influences and becomes more unique and individualized with respect to identity and attitude. A person thereby attains a degree of uniqueness with a specific selection of attitudes, preferences, tastes and characteristics. This is the person we know as a singular friend or partner, totally unique and irreplaceable and with a distinct identity and personality. Thus the individual reaches a state of distinctiveness, which is the signature of personality.

Meanwhile, through this process of separation many aspects of the self have been left out or not fully developed in order to achieve a level of distinc-tiveness. Some aspects of the potential personality, which are embedded in the self, have never seen the light of day at all and remain purely latent. These may emerge spontaneously into consciousness first in the form of symbolic figures in dreams or they may show themselves in projections. Thus shadow and anima or animus come to us in the course of time and eventually offer themselves, or demand, to be recognized. The psyche offers them for integra-tion into the conscious personality. If this is accomplished, these newly emer-gent aspects of the self are important in modifying identity and sense of self. This is the second movement of individuation, the movement of integration. Both are necessary for full incarnation. The first builds ego and sharpens conscious identity; the second includes more and more of the potential personality and builds toward a fuller incarnation of the self.

For the project of integration, or fuller incarnation of the self, which normally sets in more actively in the second half of life, it is necessary to employ a part of the mind and a kind of thinking that I will designate as "lunar". This is not analytic but rather imaginative thinking, a type of thinking that poets and artists employ regularly and all of us use without knowing it when we make quick judgments and follow our hunches. It is a great resource for incarnation because it is able to grasp symbols and work with them, whereas the analytic mind stands helpless and puzzled before them and often tries to make sense of them by dividing and subdividing, by cutting them to pieces and actually damaging or destroying them rather than making their hidden contents more available to consciousness for integration. Culturally, we owe an inestimable debt of gratitude to the poets and artists because they present symbols to culture for integration into collective consciousness. On a personal level, we must all become artists in a sense in order to facilitate the full incarnation of the self.

Jung wrote explicitly about these two types of thinking as directed and fantasy thinking (Jung 1912/1970: paras. 4-46). He had in mind what we might today recognize as the difference between left-brain analytical thinking and right-brain imaginal thinking. In his day, he did not have access to the neuroscientific findings that confirm that the human brain does indeed allow for these two distinct types of mental operation. The brain works differently in each hemisphere. In addition, we now know quite a lot about the sleeping/ dreaming brain, which shows imaginal and associative thinking processes at work similar to those of right brain activity, but with different chemicals suffusing the neurons from those of the waking brain. Right brain thinking while awake and dream thinking while we are asleep overlap in quality and so can be considered related, especially when fantasy thinking takes place spontaneously and not asked for, arising in a state of relatively unfocused consciousness.

Several years after writing about the distinction between the two types of thinking, Jung decided to engage deliberately in fantasy thinking and from this arose the material that forms the basis of his highly original and imaginal work, *The Red Book* (Jung 2009). There he speaks extensively about the difference between "the Spirit of the Times" and "the Spirit of the Depths". The first is adapted to one's outer social and cultural context and focused on practical and survival issues; the second is linked to spiritual and instinctual issues. This distinction breaks along similar lines to the difference between "directed thinking" and "fantasy thinking". In *The Red Book*, we see Jung connecting the two types of thinking and using both. With the one he engages in active imagination and with the other he performs cognitive operations on the images thus obtained in order to interpret and understand them. He also draws some dreams into the picture and weaves them into the narrative of his imaginal productions. In this, he is building a bridge between them in order to integrate them. He calls this bridge "the transcendent function" (Jung 1916/1969).

In using the term "lunar mind", I am referencing a combination of: a) the sleeping mind at work as it dreams us, and b) the (probably mostly) right brain activity we know as active imagination or thinking in images and stories.

The dreaming mind like the awake, imagining mind is more emotional and imagistic than analytic and reflective. The lunar mind works in the colors of emotion and creates scenes and stories based on associations and deep memories as well as unconscious archetypal patterns. It is almost devoid of analytic thinking and rational reflection as we know these functions in conscious waking life. In Jung's early work, he shows the typical modern cultural prejudice in favor of analytical thinking, which regards imaginal or fantasy thinking as inferior. It is not scientific. The lunar mind also pays little attention to linear sequencing, and in dreaming, it has been established, declarative memory (memory that is attained quickly and consciously) is attenuated. The lunar mind is a mind at work, nevertheless, and busy with many important activities that benefit our well-being directly and indirectly and indeed ensure our survival. J. Allan Hobson, the neuroscientist who has studied the dreaming brain perhaps most extensively, concludes that:

> Our dreams are emotional, and something that psychologists term 'hyper-associative', because our brains are activated by cholinergic rather than aminergic chemicals. Thus, we restore the most fundamental aspects of our cognitive capability – the capacity to order our memories in a way that serves survival. Emotional salience or relevance is a general mnemonic rule. Our level of emotional competence has a high survival value and underlies the more precise information needed to function socially. In other words, we need, first and foremost, to know when to approach, when to mate, when to be afraid, and when to run for cover. These are the skills that sleep refreshes every night of our lives by activating our brains, with no regard for the details of declarative memory (memory that is learned quickly and consciously). As with thermoregulation, and immunity to infection, our instincts to flee, fight, feed, and fornicate are crucial to survival and to procreation.
>
> (Hobson 2002: 88)

The dreaming mind is closer to archetype and instinct than is the waking mind, and this is true for the lunar mind as well.

Moreover, the dreaming mind is autonomous and free of the waking ego's controlling influences. In dreams, the "I" figure is one character among others in the dramas, not the controlling center. In normal waking consciousness, the ego's position is quite different, usually central. In what we may call solar consciousness, to distinguish it from lunar consciousness, the ego is the center of consciousness and holds the levers of control. Of course, this is somewhat illusory, since the decisions that the ego takes in specific circumstances are often under the strong influence of various complexes in the background. Solar consciousness tends to be focused, and it includes analytic functions and has ready access to declarative memory. It can proceed by directed logical thinking rather than by association, metaphor, and image. In the solar world, the ego can make plans and execute them since it has control over the motoric system and can direct it to carry out commands. In the lunar mind, the ego is more subject to other psychic forces and does not appear to be as able to control them. This is also true for right brain fantasy thinking, as novelists often attest and say that their fictional characters take over after a certain point, though this is less so the case than it is for dreaming where the ego really is often helpless.

In alchemy, Sol and Luna are brother and sister. For depth psychology, solar and lunar minds are seen as complimentary aspects of a single entity, the mind as a whole.

The type of interpersonal field that analysts speak of in reference to their clinical practice is partially, but only partially, under the control of solar consciousness. It is also willfully open to the vagaries of the lunar mind, which is the musing, containing mind in a state of reverie. The interpersonal field of relationship often takes on a dreamlike quality, ebbing and flowing, proceeding by association rather than rational thought, playful with metaphor, open to the unconscious and its emergent phenomena. Especially when dreams are introduced into the field is this true. The dream can have a contagious effect and induce a lunar field of great power and conviction that infects both people in the session. When this happens, the therapist is left wondering who is in charge of the process that is emerging and unfolding in the consulting room.

From what I have read in the literature about the science of dreaming, no one to date is able to declare who or what creates dreams. Who is the dream-maker? In a passage of *The Red Book*, Jung writes: "I awaken. The day reddens in the East. A night, a wonderful night in the distant depths of time lies behind me. In what faraway space was I? What did I dream? [*"Was träumte mir?"*]" (Jung 2009: 270). The English translation is not quite accurate here. Literally, the German text would say: "What dreamt me?" This takes us closer to Jung's view that the self and not the ego is the dream-maker. In Jung's theory, dreams are compensatory to waking consciousness and are meant to create greater wholeness in consciousness. By compensation, he does not mean opposition necessarily but rather a movement toward overcoming the inevitable one-sidedness of focused solar consciousness by filling in the gaps or adding a dimension that exists potentially within the self but is lacking in consciousness.

In Jungian psychoanalysis, we spend a good deal of time reflecting on the meaning of dreams on the assumption that they have something of value to tell us. We do this, of course, from the solar side of consciousness, fully awake. But as we engage with dreams as told by patients, we often enter into a kind of lunar reverie, a state of mind that is more amenable to symbolic messages from the self. "To concern ourselves with dreams is a way of reflecting on ourselves – a way of self-reflection", Jung explains to an audience of laypersons in Zurich. "It is not our ego-consciousness reflecting on itself; rather, it turns its attention to the objective actuality of the dream as a communication or message from the unconscious, unitary soul of humanity. It reflects not on the ego but on the self; it recollects that strange self, alien to the ego, which was ours from the beginning, the trunk from which the ego grew. It is alien to us because, through the aberrations of consciousness, we have alienated ourselves from it" (Jung 1933/1964: par. 318). The reflection on dreams leads us, therefore, into the widest possible perspective on our lives and their meaning within the context of history and the collective mind of humanity. The lunar mind connects us to life at its deepest and highest levels. Bringing lunar mind into contact with solar mind helps us to reconnect waking consciousness to its source in the self and even beyond the psychological self to the Ground of Being.

The compensatory action of the unconscious with respect to consciousness has a teleological thrust, moreover. It becomes increasingly evident as we individuate that not only the solar mind plans, anticipates and thinks about the future. The lunar mind does this as well, but from a different perspective and with another view in mind. The prospective function of the lunar mind makes contributions to consciousness that the solar mind cannot. The psyche strives to become more fully conscious and incarnated, and the dreaming mind assists in this process. The lunar mind knows of things that the solar mind does not, or does not know well enough, and brings them forward in an emotional, dramatic and highly colorful fashion in dreams, fantasies and visions. The dream-maker speaks precisely to our immediate individuation needs.

In thinking about the lunar mind, whether in its waking version as active imagination or in its sleeping version as dreaming, it is important to remain aware that we are dealing with the psyche and not merely with the brain. We are also not primarily occupied with metaphysical or metapsychological theories. Most basically, we are concerned with issues of identity, relationship, and meaning at the emotional and imaginal level. Incarnation of the self takes place within the sphere of the psyche. "The psyche is a phenomenal world in itself, which can be reduced neither to the brain nor to metaphysics", Jung declared presciently long before the dawn of the era of neuroscience (Jung 1955/1963: par. 667). This does not mean that the scientific study of the dreaming brain is irrelevant, nor is the study of metaphysics, theology, and metapsychology. But, in reality, these fall into the background as one deals with matters of incarnation of the self on a practical level.

Chapter 6

Hints of transcendence

In a letter to P.W. Martin dated August 20 1945, Jung confirmed the centrality of numinous experience in his life and work:

> I know it is exceedingly difficult to write anything definite or descriptive about the progression of psychological states. It always seemed to me as if the real milestones were certain symbolic events characterized by a strong emotional tone. You are quite right, the main interest of my work is not concerned with the treatment of neuroses but rather with the approach to the numinous. But the fact is that the approach to the numinous is the real therapy and inasmuch as you attain to the numinous experiences you are released from the curse of pathology. Even the very disease takes on a numinous character.
>
> (Jung 1973: 377)

If one holds the classical Jungian view that the only genuine cure for neurosis is to grow out of it through pursuing individuation, then treatment based on this model would seem necessarily to include "the approach to the numinous", as Jung states so firmly in this letter. The individuation process, or incarnation of the self as I am calling it, typically includes experiences of a numinous nature.

The question is: How are such momentous experiences related to and used, and how do they contribute to the overall process of individuation? We may begin to answer this question by considering how numinous experiences release a person from the curse of pathology, as Jung claims in his letter to P.W. Martin. Generally speaking, an "approach to the numinous" is considered a religious undertaking, a pilgrimage. The "attainment to the numinous experiences" that Jung speaks of refers to religious experiences of a quasi-mystical nature. Such experiences may well persuade a person that life is meaningful. Numinous experience can create a convincing link to the transcendent, to the Ground of Being, the Divinity beyond the individual psyche and soul, and this may well lead to the feeling that character flaws like addictions or behavioral disorders are trivial by comparison with the grand visions imparted in the mystical state. The pathological symptom can even be seen in retrospect as an incitement to go on the spiritual quest, or even as a paradoxical doorway into transcendence, and this can donate meaning to the malady itself. Perhaps some degree of pathology is needed, in fact, in order for a person to feel strongly motivated to set out on a spiritual quest to begin with. In this case, attainment to numinous experiences would bring about a change in the feeling that pathology is a curse, even if it did not result in curing the pathology itself, although it might lead to this as well.

However, for modern and psychologically astute people, such a spiritual awakening might signify only a temporary easing rather than a definitive solution to the deep structural problems created by neurosis. For such people, who tend to be the ones who seek out psychoanalysis rather than spiritual guidance, spiritual awareness by itself is not enough. So how could the attainment to numinous experiences contribute to the more far-reaching psychological project of individuation? This is a more complicated problem.

Incarnation of the self has to do with living a full life and realizing all the potentials inherent in the self. Going on spiritual quests and having numinous experiences may be part of the route to individuation, but by themselves they are not enough to establish, let alone to complete, an individuation process, although they may create a profound change in attitude and personality, as in the case of Saul of Tarsus who undergoes such a far-reaching transformation of attitude on the road to Damascus that it changes his entire life's course. But even in Paul's case, the numinous experience on the road to Damascus is only the beginning of his further development. Much remains for him to undergo and to integrate before he can achieve a full incarnation of the self. We see his further individuation struggles clearly in the Epistles.

Generally speaking, a numinous experience is a "hint" of the transcendent Ground of Being that lies beyond our limited psyche, but it is filtered through our psyches via the lunar mind to consciousness. It is a hint that larger, non-egoic powers exist in and beyond the psyche that need to be considered and ultimately brought into relationship with consciousness. Numinous experience is a type of extraordinary manifestation through the lunar mind of unconscious figures and processes. Like the dream, it brings a needed compensation to consciousness.

Because Jung weighted numinous experience with such great significance for individuation, it is instructive to know something about this terminology and where it came from. The German theologian Rudolf Otto (1869-1937) created the term *numinosum* and also its derivatives "numinous" and "numinosity" in his famous work, *Das Heilige* (translated into English, somewhat unfortunately, as *The Idea of the Holy*), in order to describe "the Holy" in such a way as to keep it distinct from other theological and philosophical or ethical concepts, such as "the good" or "goodness". He writes: "For this purpose I adopt a word coined from the Latin *numen*. *Omen* has given us 'ominous', and there is no reason why from *numen* we should not similarly form a word 'numinous'" (Otto 1917/1950: 6-7). Otto wanted moreover to describe the human experience of "the Holy", not the theological concept of holiness. His work introduced a strong psychological and emotional component into the study of religion, which stood in marked contrast to other comparative and historical approaches and above all to the theological, which generally speaks almost exclusively for received doctrines and offers a rational (in the sense of an organized and systematic) explication of traditional teachings and texts (i.e., "revelation"). Otto, on the contrary, wanted to speak about the nature of religious experience and to demonstrate the fundamental importance of the irrational in religion, hence his book's subtitle: *"Über das Irrationale in der Idee des Göttlichen und sein Verhältnis zum Rationalen"* ("On the Irrational in the Idea of the Divine and its Relation to the Rational"). While not arguing to abandon the rational elements of theology totally (Otto 1917/1950: 1-4), Otto did powerfully set forth the nonrational quality of religious experience and especially its strong emotional overtones. For him, the human encounter with "the Holy", as image, ritual, or sound, could only be accurately described with strong words like *mysterium tremendum et fascinans* (an awe-full and fascinating mystery), a phrase that he explicates meticulously and profoundly in his exposition of numinous experience. To enter into the presence of "the Holy" was for him to be shaken to the foundations by the power and awesome magnitude of the Other who is confronted in this experience. To describe this, he uses words like "shudder", "stupor", "astonishment", and "blank wonder". As a student of the world's mysticisms, he also related this to the "void" of Buddhist mystics (Otto 1917/1950: 30). This universal religious moment is primarily an experience of the lunar mind heavily loaded with emotion, whereas theology is above all an exercise in solar thinking and reflection.

It is not altogether clear how Otto arrived at his conviction about the centrality of the numinous in religion, whether through the influence of early teachers and ministers, or of philosophers like Kant and Fries whom he studied deeply, or from Christian theologians like Schleiermacher who also emphasized the crucial importance of feeling in religious life and teaching, or by taking into account his own experiences of the Holy (Alles 1996: 62-63). Whatever the reasons, he was urgently gripped and utterly fascinated by the power of numinous experience. In his letters written back home during his travels, he describes two impressive incidents that some scholars have regarded as decisive for his deep appreciation of the numinous. These offer a vivid account of what he means by "numinous experience" (Alles 1996: 80-81; 94-95). Here we find the religious shudder and the strong emotional response that Otto will later analyze in *Das Heilige*. This memorable experience must at the minimum have contributed importantly to the experiential ground for writing about the numinous with personal conviction. These deeply-moving experiences within religious traditions not his own (one Jewish and the other Hindu) contributed to Otto's conviction that all religions are founded upon such strong impressions of "the Holy."

The spiritual ground beneath the temples and the cathedrals of all religions, supporting their rites and rituals and their Sacred Scriptures, is made of numinous experiences, and is therefore psychological. For Otto, this forms the universal, foundational bedrock of all world religions: "From the very beginning religion is experience of the Mysterium, of what breaks forth from the depths of our life of feeling... as the feeling of the supersensual" (Alles 1996: 52, n. 44). Otto's grounding of religion in the experience of the Mysterium was fully compatible with Jung's view: "The idea of God originated with the experience of the numinosum. It was a psychical experience, with moments when man felt overcome. Rudolf Otto has designated this moment in his Psychology of Religion as the numinosum, which is derived from the Latin *numen*, meaning hint, or sign" (Jung 1988: 1038).

As a student of world religions, Otto could see the universality of humankind's experience of the *numinosum*. Since time immemorial, humans have noted the "feeling of the supersensual" that Otto refers to in his definition. This is the experiential basis of religions, high and low, near and far. All are on an equal footing in this respect. Appreciating the value of religious experience universally, he was freed from the narrow confines of his orthodox Lutheranism and, as a result, he entered energetically and enthusiastically into dialogue with members of other religious communities, founded a "Religious League of Humanity", and proposed a parliament of world religions to be "made up of official representatives of the various religions" (Alles 1996: 147). For his liberal attitude he paid a high price at home in his German university at Marburg, where he received harsh and even abusive criticism and ridicule from the neo-orthodox Christian students and a variety of other theologians, but his project was to create a vision for the appreciation of religious experience as a universal human phenomenon. For Jung, this would be evidence for a "religious instinct", which with the other instincts and psychic impulses moves the individual toward incarnation of the self.

Jung's concern with healing and with the psychological process of individuation was quite other than Otto's primary focus, which was exclusively centered on the religious aspects of life and on worship of the Holy. Jung, on the other hand, personally engaged the experience of Divinity as a psychological opus. The passion for the spiritual, like other passions, can easily tip over into pathos and extreme alienation of other parts of the self. The goal of individuation, unlike that of the mystical quest, is not to lose oneself in the Divinity but in the forging of the polarities inherent in the self into an image of unity and integrating this into consciousness.

"It is altogether amazing how little most people reflect on numinous objects and attempt to come to terms with them", Jung exclaims in his famous theological outburst, *Answer to Job*, "and how laborious such an undertaking is once we have embarked upon it. The numinosity of the object makes it difficult to handle intellectually, since our affectivity is always involved" (Jung 1954/1969: para. 735). Integration of this type of experience is a difficult task but absolutely essential to the *opus* of incarnation of the full self.

In Jung's analysis, the problem of the polarities (good/evil, masculine/feminine) within the Biblical God-image was brought to a climax in the Book of Job and later in the Book of Revelation, then passed on to the alchemists and Cabalists who attempted to resolve the opposites in a *mysterium coniunctionis*, and finally handed over to psychology where the individuation process is dedicated to the opus.

Chapter 7

Turning on the transcendent function

Something strange and uncanny happens when one becomes deeply engaged with living symbols. Karl Barth, the great Protestant theologian of the twentieth century, wrote in a letter to a friend that while he was most intensely engaged in his study of the Holy Trinity and with placing this Christian symbol at the center of his multi-volume *Church Dogmatics*, he had an unsettling experience. "All this past week", he wrote, "I have repeatedly pulled my hair wondering how this would all be possible: recently I woke up suddenly in the middle of the night because I dreamed so very vividly about the scandalous subjectivity of this revelation, which somehow was literally (and unfortunately also objectively!!) coming towards me, when suddenly the wind ripped open the door of the room and slammed shut the window (in reality), so that the racket and the dogmatic vision miraculously came together" (Schildmann 1991/2006: 171 – my translation). As Wolfgang Schildmann, a Berlin Jungian psychoanalyst and close student of the relation between Barth's dreams and his theological works, comments: "His 'melancholy' brooding over the ancient runes of dogma, his numinous dream experience with synchronistic accompaniment, and his feeling that he must follow his inner necessity confirms Jung's opinion that the Trinitarian developmental process has to do with 'fateful transformations' that 'as a rule have a numinous character'" (Schildmann 1991/2006: 181 – my translation). Barth's deep broodings on a religious symbol were here accompanied by numinous and synchronistic events in his experienced world. The dreaming lunar mind connected with the physical world to create a moment of transcendence. Subjectivity and objectivity coincided in a meaningful way in this experience and pointed to the archetype behind the phenomena.

To our modern and postmodern mentality this view of the synchronistic experience would most likely be written off to a momentary cultural lapse, a regression. On the other hand, as David Tacey has written in his trenchant paper, 'Imagining transcendence at the end of modernity', the "return of the religious [in the postmodern era] has nothing to do with reactionary reassertion of religious truth and doctrine"; instead, it is about the "recovery of our relationship with the sacred after the collapse of positivistic science and after loss of belief in theistic religion and absolute truth" (Tacey 2008: 65). So it may be that we are here approaching the breaking point of modernity and making way for a very different type of spirituality and mentality than has been known before.

The question here will be: How are experiences of transcendence brought into the incarnational project of individuation? Do they make a difference?

Jung, a fellow Basler and an almost exact contemporary of Karl Barth's, reports several experiences quite similar to the Protestant theologian's. In each of these we find three converging vertices: 1) a conscious preoccupation with an archetypal image (the conscious vertex); 2) a dream or a vision (an unconscious vertex); and 3) a corresponding external phenomenon (an objective vertex) (Figure 7.1).

The three vertices establish a nexus of associations that is anchored in the subject's life at the moment. The burden will then be on the subject to make use of the experience for incarnational purposes.

In one instance, this convergence occurred to Jung in relation to his preoccupation with the Christ symbol. "In 1939 I gave a seminar on the *Spiritual Exercises* of Ignatius Loyola", he writes in *Memories, Dreams, Reflections*. "One night I awoke and saw, bathed in bright light at the foot of my bed, the figure of Christ on the Cross. It was not quite life-size, but extremely distinct; and I saw that his body was made of greenish gold. The vision was marvelously beautiful, and yet I was profoundly shaken by it" (Jung 1963a: 210). Similar to Karl Barth's experience, an unconscious image was constellated by intensive study of a religious symbol.

Jung continues in his autobiography by reporting a number of other dreams related to his steady and intense preoccupation with Christian religious imagery including, most importantly, the fish symbol. After the dream of the

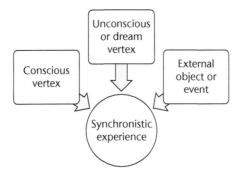

Figure 7.1 Three converging vertices.

green Christ image, he continued writing about Christian symbols and themes in essays on the Roman Catholic Mass (Jung 1941/1969), on the Trinity (Jung 1942/1969), and on Christ as a symbol of the self in his large-scale work, *Aion* (Jung 1950/1968). In 1949, ten years after the vision of Christ at the foot of his bed and while again deeply immersed in the study of Christ as a symbol of the self and of the Christian tradition over the last two millennia and its relation to the astrological Age of Pisces – so, of course, while in a state of brooding over the meaning of the fish symbol – he made the following observation in his diary:

> I noted the following on April 1, 1949. Today is Friday. We have fish for lunch. Somebody happens to mention the custom of making an 'April fish' of someone. That same morning I made a note of an inscription which read: 'Est homo totus medius *piscis* ab imo.' In the afternoon a former patient of mine, whom I had not seen for months, showed me some extremely impressive pictures of fish, which she had painted in the meantime. In the evening I was shown a piece of embroidery with fish-like sea-monsters in it. On the morning of April 2 another patient, whom I had not seen for many years, told me a dream in which she stood on the shore of a lake and saw a large fish that swam straight towards her and landed at her feet. I was at this time engaged on a study of the fish symbol in history.
>
> (Jung 1952/1969: para. 826)

These objects constitute the third vertex.

Actually, the objects conceal a hidden "fourth" element, which opens a window to transcendence. The contents of the third vertex bear closer scrutiny. They belong to the world beyond the psyche and therefore introduce an element into the experience of synchronicity that lies outside of or beyond the realm of subjectivity. The other two vertices – conscious thoughts and preoccupations on the one hand and images from dreams and visions on the other – are mental and of a psychic nature. The first resides in the solar mind, the second in the lunar. They are embedded in the psychic matrix, and one cannot be sure to what extent or how accurately they reflect anything beyond. Epistemological caution advises us not to assume naively that they reflect objective reality. But the third vertex brings in objects that exist outside of the psychic matrix. Moreover, the contents of this vertex are dual in the sense that they have an intimate relationship with the subjective and psychic realm on the one side (they are identical with the images being contemplated in consciousness and symbolized in dreams or visions) and yet are radically and completely independent of the psychic matrix on the other. These are objects that mirror the subject and participate in the psychic realm intimately, but they are not determined, created, or dependent on the subject. In Barth's case, this was the wind that opened the door and slammed the window; in Jung's, it was the fish. This strange object is a symbol, therefore, that is a metaphor but more than that. It manages to transcend both subject and object and unite them. It is a bridge.

In his early paper, 'The Transcendent Function', Jung writes about a psychic bridging function between conscious and unconscious (vertices 1 and 2): "There is nothing mysterious or metaphysical about the term 'transcendent function.' It means a psychological function comparable in its way to a mathematical function of the same name, which is a function of real and imaginary numbers. The psychological 'transcendent function' arises from the union of conscious and unconscious contents" (Jung 1916/1969: para. 131, n.1). This was written before he had developed the theory of synchronicity and the notion of "transgressivity" of the archetypes. In the early paper, he wants to state strongly that the term transcendent function is strictly limited to the psychological realm (vertices 1 and 2) without any reference to what I am calling the synchronistic vertex. This was an early statement and based on his interests and understandings at the time. The transcendent function as he thought of it in 1916 is nothing more and nothing less than a combination of conscious and unconscious contents, a melding of solar and lunar minds' contents. It is a product of the work done by delving into and bringing to the surface and integrating material that lies in the unconscious, either because of repression (the shadow, primarily) or because it has not yet been symbolized sufficiently to make itself available to consciousness but which now, thanks to a dream or vision or active imagination, has become available and can be integrated into consciousness as part of a new and expanded sense of self. This is of course at the heart of the project of incarnating the self. The transcendent function in this understanding is a crafted identity formation that gradually comes into being through inner work and integration. Eventually this identity exceeds the purely personal history of the individual because it also contains archetypal material and imagery. The transcendent function typically contains archetypal images and energies and thus moves an individual's identity onto a partially symbolic level. It offers an identity based on historical and imaginal contents. This is generally seen as an optimal outcome of the individuation process as fostered and augmented through prolonged engagement in Jungian psychoanalysis and continuous inner work thereafter. It is beautifully illustrated in *The Red Book*.

What is missing in this picture and what Jung adds piece by piece later over the course of several decades is a spiritual element, which is and is not psychic, both personal and impersonal, individual soul and soul of the world (*anima mundi*). This would be expressed in symbols that are not limited to the psychic realm, conscious or unconscious. If these are included in the incarnational process, the transcendent function in this version is no longer limited to the psychological domain. A divine element, which is embedded within the human but is not strictly speaking of the human or limited to the human, is additionally captured in this later understanding of the transcendent. It is a spiritual element and transcendent to the psyche.

What does strong transcendence mean for the subject, for the person experiencing it? What does it add to the incarnational process of individuation? It brings the lived realization that there is an ontological ground under this process that extends beyond the limits of the individual, even beyond death. The Divinity, or Ground of Being, is made manifest and becomes incarnated in consciousness, or consciousness in it. This is an objective reality in which the subject is privileged to participate and which extends far beyond the dimensions of a particular human individual into the *unus mundus* and to Divinity itself.

Chapter 8

Not just a butterfly

The opportunity to experience true transcendence doubtless occurs much more often than we commonly realize. It is likely that we are exposed to synchronistic events on a daily basis without noticing them. Perhaps the most tragic failure of human consciousness is that it so easily misses what is untoward and unusual. Mostly we see only what we expect or want to see. We are so focused on our immediate tasks and projects that we pay scant attention to what is going on at the fringes. If we do notice a surprising coincidence here and there – the near miss of a fatal accident, the surprise of picking up the phone to call someone when it rings and that very person is calling us, or a dream suddenly corresponding to an event in waking life the next day – we do not take the time to reflect deeply on the meaning tucked into it. Occasionally, though, a cluster of synchronicities surrounds us so auspiciously and convincingly that it grabs our attention. We are astonished by the sound of invisible wings and perhaps shudder at the uncanny presences in our midst.

Moments in life that are charged with intense emotion are often the occasion for such vivid synchronicities. We are more likely then to be observant. When we stand squarely in the presence of death, for example, especially of a loved one, our senses seem to be more attuned to hints of transcendence. Our intuitive antennae are extended and on alert.

I offer an example. Several years ago a dear friend of mine passed away. I knew Sister Irene for over ten years, first as a client and then later as a delightfully pleasant conversation partner and friend. In the course of this time, she told me a lot about her life, her emotional responses to people and events in the past and in the present, her dreams and expectations. Now at the end of a long life and productive life, she was in the process of summing up and putting her memories in order. Irene had been a Catholic nun for her entire adult life, and she believed without reservation in the reality of God and the afterlife, but she held these beliefs with a light hand and a twinkle in her eye. She had become crippled in her later years after spending perhaps too much time on her knees earlier – not only in prayer but in scrubbing the floors of the convent when she was young – and eventually was confined to a wheelchair. She grieved the loss of her physical mobility, and the sheer dependence on her fellow sisters in the home where she was cared for would make her angry and miserable at times. She had to bear the frustration of severely-crippled legs, but she enjoyed telling me that when she died and went to heaven the first thing she wanted to do there was to dance. She loved to imagine her body whole again and capable of full movement. This is what she looked forward to most of all, even more than to meeting dearly departed loved ones and the religiously famous. In her youth she had thrilled to music and came alive on the dance floor in her New England town. She enjoyed telling me about these happy moments with a mischievous chuckle. We would laugh together and enjoy the image.

Sometime before Irene was diagnosed with untreatable cancer and her swift decline afterwards, the Chicago newspapers ran a story saying that Pope John Paul II had confirmed the sainthood of Edith Stein and would canonize her at St Peter's Cathedral in Rome. The date was not yet set, but the ceremony was certain to take place in the near future. Edith Stein had been a heroine of mine ever since I had been introduced to her writings and life-story some years earlier, so I was thrilled to hear of this development and wondered if it would be possible to attend the service at St Peter's in Rome. Irene had excellent connections in Rome, I knew, so I asked her if she thought it would be possible for me to obtain entry to the canonization. She promised to make a phone call and later assured me that when the time came for Edith Stein's canonization I would have seats. I thanked her profusely.

After Irene received the fatal diagnosis, she died quickly, choosing to ask her doctors to withhold any type of extraordinary treatment. She was prepared to take leave of her body and to go on in the spirit to meet her Maker and the loved ones who had gone before, especially a young sister who had died at an early age so many years before. My wife and I had the privilege of being with Irene for an hour on the day before she passed away. She was in and out of consciousness and barely showed awareness of our presence, but I was quite sure she could observe us from another place in the psyche, from "up there in the corner of the room". We kissed her goodbye, wishing her a good journey through the valley of the shadow of death. I knew she was as well prepared for this final experience in life as anyone can be.

On the day of her funeral we were surprised to learn that the site of her service had been changed from the nursing home, which had a nice little chapel in it, to a much larger church, and so we had come to the wrong place and at the wrong time. The service was to be held several hours later in another part of the city. Our car was parked in a lovely garden behind the nursing home. It was an extremely hot day in Chicago, and the windows and doors had been closed tight because the interior of the car was cooled by air conditioning.

To save the cool air inside, we got in and out quickly. As we drove away, I asked my wife to check the back seat. Something must have unaccountably gotten into our car and was flapping around in the rear window. She turned to the rear window and exclaimed in surprise: "It's a butterfly!"

"Impossible," I said. "How could a butterfly have gotten into our car? The windows were closed tight!"

But, sure enough, there it was, a brown butterfly with bits of blue on its wings, as it turned out. I opened the windows offering it an escape and hoping it would fly away, but it refused to leave. It was determined to stay in the rear window of our car for the whole trip and would not take the opportunity to escape. We parked the car later at a restaurant and opened the back doors. Still the butterfly would not budge. Even after the funeral service hours later, the butterfly continued to accompany us as we drove homeward in the dark. We began to speak of it jokingly as Irene.

"Well, OK, Irene has decided to come home with us!"

When we got home my wife reached her hand into the back of the car hoping that the butterfly would now accept the invitation to make an exit. Previously this had not worked, but this time the butterfly hopped onto her hand and sat tight. We called to our friend Joyce, who was staying with our daughter and dog inside the house, to come outside and see Irene since she had known her quite well.

As we stood together outside under a streetlight, Irene-the-butterfly suddenly decided to jump to the ground where she began performing an amazing whirling dance at our feet. Round and round she danced in a dizzying frenzy of motion! Suddenly I remembered Irene's ardently-expressed wish to dance again in the afterlife, and the words burst out of me, "Well, Irene, I see you've made it! You're dancing! Bravo!"

At that moment, the boundaries between this world and the next were breached. I could only feel that in this moment we occupied a realm that existed both in time and eternity. Surely this was Irene dancing before us right here on the ground in the form of a butterfly, but she danced as well in another world at the same time. The butterfly, and we too momentarily, occupied both dimensions at once.

Then the butterfly flew away and disappeared. We remained stunned, and we knew we had witnessed something truly extraordinary.

The next morning our friend, Joyce, telephoned. She said: "Guess what happened to the butterfly we saw last night!"

"What?" I asked in surprise.

"It came home with me in my car! When I got home, there it was in the back window. I let it out of the car and it flew off in the direction of Dorothy's garden." Dorothy lived a few blocks away and had been one of Irene's best friends for half a century.

The experience was indelibly inscribed in all of our memories. We spoke of Irene often afterwards and observed other synchronicities, like a large moving truck with her family name painted on the side of it passing while we stood casually chatting in remembrance of her.

Then about a year passed when I learned of the date of Edith Stein's canonization in Rome. Thanks to Irene's earlier intervention with her friends in the Eternal City, I was able to get tickets from the Vatican. The ceremony took place in St Peter's Square on October 11, 1998.

I had been fascinated by the story of Edith Stein's life for some years. She was born into a Jewish family in a city now in Poland, and in her twenties she converted to Roman Catholicism, much to the consternation of her mother. She had previously studied philosophy with Edmund Husserl in Freiburg, Germany and wrote a highly-regarded dissertation on the subject of empathy. As a Catholic nun, she became a well-known spokeswoman for women in the Catholic Church during the 1920s and traveled throughout Germany lecturing and teaching. It seems, though, that her main passion was for the mystical. In the 1930s, she was allowed to join the order of the Carmelites and entered the seclusion of a cloistered life devoted entirely to contemplation and prayer. When the war broke out and Nazi persecution of Jews in Germany intensified even beyond its previous extremes, she was quietly transferred from Cologne to Amsterdam out of concern for her safety, but her safety there was short-lived. In 1942 she, along with all the other known Jews in The Netherlands, was rounded up and carried off in the night by train to their horrible destination in the death camps. Although she was offered the opportunity to leave the convoy and be taken to Switzerland and safety, she would not leave her people and so she died with so many others in Auschwitz.

I was interested in her life for many reasons and had read some of her works and several biographies. In addition, I had never witnessed a canonization service before. So I was in a state of high anticipation as my wife and I and a couple of Roman friends made our way to the choice seats reserved for us, thanks to the help of Irene and her connections in Rome.

The service was, unsurprisingly, very moving. The aged Pope, by then so bent and weakened by age and physical disabilities, made his way slowly out of the doors of the cathedral to his chair on the platform in the front of St Peter's Square and from there presided for three hours over a service that was obviously special for him. Both he and Edith Stein were from Poland. He had been committed for years to healing the ancient conflict between Christians and Jews and was the first Roman Catholic Pope ever to visit a synagogue in Rome. In St Peter's Square that day, the ritual, the music, the crowd of 70,000 people from all parts of the world, and the illustrious cardinals and politicians on the platform with the Pope, all contributed to create an impressive effect. In that atmosphere, the sense of an invisible world surrounding and hovering over us became quite palpable. It was a religious experience in the best sense of the word.

But nothing prepared me for what happened as the service was drawing to a close. We were standing in the warm sun for the final prayer of benediction as the Pope began intoning his closing blessing in Latin. The printed text of this prayer, which was contained in a booklet handed out to everyone at the beginning of the service, was presented in four languages, and I was following the Pope's unclear diction as best I could understand it. When he arrived at the line, "*Ex hoc nunc et usque in saeculum*", – "*Von nun an bis in Ewigkeit*", "*Ora e sempre*", "Now and forever", an utterly astonishing thing happened. A brown butterfly with blue bits of color on its wings appeared out of nowhere from that crowd of thousands and alighted on the open page. It perched quietly on the words "*Ora e sempre*" and stayed put there without a flicker.

At first, I could not apprehend. What was happening right here in front of me? The appearance of this butterfly on my book came as a total and shocking surprise. I had seen no butterflies in that sea of human faces. There were none there, I was sure of it. It was impossible. I was stunned. No room here for irony. It was sheer astonishment. Where had this butterfly come from? We were in the middle of a veritable sea of humanity and in the middle of a gigantic city covered in concrete and stone, not in a garden.

My wife looked over at my book and whispered: "It's the same, the butterfly we saw in Chicago!" Sure enough, the colors were the same. Our friends beside us, who did not know the previous story of Irene the butterfly and so did not register the same awareness, were however also amazed to see a butterfly in this unlikely place and sitting on my book.

Can this be Irene? A sign? I wondered to myself in amazement.

The butterfly lifted off the page and took to the air as the Pope said "Amen" and disappeared in the direction of the altar some 50 meters in front of us. My thought was that it joined the other spirits and angels so palpably present in Piazza San Pietro that bright day in October.

Now if we think about what kind of an object this butterfly is, its duality is irrefutable. Literally, it is a biological object of the Lepidoptera order; at the same time, it is an object of a spiritual order, or what I think of as Irene's spirit or a symbol of her spirit. In the physical butterfly, I registered Irene's spiritual presence. One can distinguish at least four elements in this picture: a) my conscious self as witness of the phenomenon, b) my mental memory image of Irene, c) the physical butterfly, and d) the spiritual entity as an invisible fourth. With the timing of its appearance, the butterfly addressed me as Irene's spirit. The kind of knowledge gained from an experience like this cannot be confirmed by tests or replicated under laboratory conditions. Do butterflies appear every time someone significant has died? No. Will a similar experience ever take place again, another butterfly? I don't know but would not count on it. But I know it once happened and I know it impressed me profoundly. This knowledge is a kind of gnosis, magic without a magician, a privileged personal awareness of an invisible spiritual presence. It is a hint of a transcendent order of being.

"Transcendence is a delirious rupture in immanence," writes theologian Regina Schwartz, "an erotic claim made by it, a gap in the Real, a question put to subjectivity, a realm of the impossible that breaks into possibility" (Schwartz 2004: xi). I am left with an indelible conviction that transcendence, in the strong sense of the word, was revealed to me in the delicate, hovering, erotic, and delightful dance of Irene the butterfly.

Chapter 9

Spirituality in the psychoanalytic context

Psychoanalysis is a child of modernity. Peter Homans (1995) has written about the cultural conditions that gave rise to the profession and the social context of the founders. In a sense, the psychoanalytic way replaced the religious for Freud and Jung and gave them comfort and sustenance in their explorations. It is often overlooked that only a generation or two separated them from established religious traditions. Freud's grandparents were Hasidic Jews, and Jung's father and maternal grandfather were Swiss Reformed clergymen. What the forefathers learned and experienced in their religious traditions, the sons and grandsons rediscovered in their own way in the realm of the psyche.

The images and symbols generated by the unconscious in dreams and fantasies echo memories of lost religious worlds. These intimations were tellingly represented in the founders' psychoanalytic working spaces. In Freud's case, this is indicated in his famous collection of small antiquities. Ana-Maria Rizzuto, a scholar of psychoanalysis, comments on these "sacred objects" in Freud's consulting rooms: "They offered him what God offers to the believer: the assurance of a constant presence and the joy of sublimated emotional contact with the enticing father... they were always there as a needed presence serving the same function that God's presence has for the believer" (Rizzuto 1998: 259). Rizzuto finds the reference to Divinity surprisingly close to the founder of psychoanalysis. Yosef Hayim Yerushalmi concludes his brilliant study of Freud's relationship to his Jewish heritage, *Freud's Moses*, with the following insight: "The Freudian integration of the personality demands the return of the repressed for the sake of new insight, as a result of which we do not have to deny our fathers but can at least attempt to reestablish our relationship on a different plane. Spring up, O well, sing ye unto it, Jakob Freud had written in 1891. From 1934 almost to his death the son drank from that well and sang to it. His song was one that the father would surely not have recognized and would perhaps have found discordant. Yet, somehow, in the balance, I feel he would not have been displeased" (Yerushalmi 1991: 79).

Jung's bow to religious tradition is also evident in his private study. There he installed stained glass windows from a medieval church in Germany

(Stiftung 2009: 6) and hung a copy of the shroud of Turin across from his writing desk. Jung's psychological theory itself can be read as a version of biblical theology. The theory of synchronicity, for example, is Jung's restatement of the familiar Protestant doctrine of Divine Providence (Stein 1995). Jung became acutely aware of the spiritual dimension of psychoanalysis and reflected on it extensively in his later writings.

However, the term "spirituality" must be understood differently in the context of psychoanalysis from what it usually means when used within traditional religious discourse. We can come closer to what spirituality means in psychoanalytic terms by taking a short detour and reflecting psychologically on a short story called 'The God's Script' by the Argentinean writer, Jorge Luis Borges.

The story tells of a Mayan priest named Tzinacan, who was captured by the Spaniard Pedro de Alvarado, tortured for a confession, and finally permanently imprisoned in a deep underground dungeon. This prison is divided into two sections. On the one side lives Tzinacan, on the other a jaguar, an animal sacred to the native peoples of the Americas. The sections are separated by a stone wall that reaches to the top of the vault. Placed in the wall is a window with bars through which Tzinacan can see the jaguar when light penetrates the space. For just a moment each day, at noon, bright sunlight enters the cell from above, as the jailer lowers the daily ration of food and water. During this brief time, Tzinacan can observe the spotted jaguar, and over the years he disciplines himself to study the pacing animal and to discern the pattern of its markings. Tzinacan believes that the High God's secret code words are inscribed in the markings on the jaguar. Whoever learns and deciphers this code will become as powerful as the God Himself. If he, Tzinacan, can come to understand the code inscribed on the jaguar, he will understand God's mind, and with this knowledge he will be able to free himself, to avenge himself against Pedro de Alvarado, and to restore his traditional religion and his tribe to greatness. Tzinacan dedicates himself to this mission.

For many years Tzinacan studies the spotted jaguar. He and the jailor grow old together. He loses his posture and his health, and eventually he becomes too weak even to raise himself up from the stone floor. Then one day he has a dream. In the dream he notices a single grain of sand in his cell. He notes this and (still within the dream) he goes to sleep again. Again he dreams, and now there are two grains of sand in his cell. A third time he goes to sleep and again he dreams of yet another grain of sand, on and on, until the grains of sand entirely fill his cell to the very top and he is suffocating and dying under their weight. He realizes that he must try to wake himself up, but as he awakens from one dream he discovers that he must awaken from yet another dream and another, on and on. In order to awaken fully he must reverse the entire immense sequence of dreams. The task looks hopeless. He will never be able to awaken from all of them.

Then suddenly, the door opens high above him and sunlight floods into the cell. Tzinacan wakes up from his nightmare. So greatly relieved is he that he blesses his jailor for opening the window and letting the light in. He even blesses this awful cell for housing him, and he blesses his old suffering body for its endurance and stamina. He is supremely grateful for his life as it is. In this instant, he becomes totally enlightened: he sees God, and he glimpses ultimate reality. What he sees is the image of a wheel made of fire and water that fills the whole cosmos and links everything that exists. Tzinacan suddenly realizes how small he is in the great scheme of things, that he is no more than one small fiber in the great fabric of being. Pedro de Alvarado, moreover, is also a fiber in the same fabric. As he studies this cosmic wheel further and comes to understand its full implications, he realizes that he now can read the script written on the coat of the jaguar. The code suddenly becomes intelligible to him. It is a formula of 14 words that, if spoken aloud, will give him all the power he needs to accomplish everything he has been desiring during this long exile in misery. At last he holds in his hand the power to abolish his prison, to renew his body, to destroy his enemy, to restore his people and their religion, and to rule as Montezuma once ruled over all of Mexico. He can fulfill his every wish!

> Forty syllables, fourteen words, and I, Tzinacan, would rule… But I know I shall never say those words, because I no longer remember Tzinacan… Whoever has seen the universe, whoever has beheld the fiery designs of the universe, cannot think in terms of one man, of that man's trivial fortunes or misfortunes, though he be that very man. That man has been he and now no more matters to him.
>
> (Borges 1964: 173)

Like the biblical Job who also fell silent when he saw the awesome majesty of God, Tzinacan seals his lips and accepts his infinitely small place in the high wheel of ultimate reality. He does not utter the "God words" because his ego has seen the self, of which it is but a tiny sliver. The ego has found its correct place in the framework of the self and lets go of its own plans and immediate desires.

Psychoanalysis is also, in an important sense, a quest to perceive the script encoded on the jaguar that we name the unconscious, to glimpse the relation of the individual to the greater self and the Divinity of which it is a reflection. Scrutinizing the mind for patterns and attempting to decipher its deep code have been central to psychoanalysis since Freud published *The Interpretation of Dreams*. It also takes place within the sealed-off space of the analytic frame, a kind of underground temenos if not prison.

It is somewhat ironic that despite his determination to keep psychoanalysis high and dry above the murky regions of occultism, esoteric wisdom, gnosis, magic, and mystical experience, Freud actually opened the door by accident to the realm of spirit when he suspended directed thinking in favor of free association and dream images. The "flood of occultism" that he warned Jung against (Jung 1963a: 150) could not be kept entirely at bay. From the beginning of the psychoanalytic movement, artists, poets, theologians, philosophers and other non-scientific and non-medically trained (or biased) people have taken part in its practice and theory building. They have been drawn to it not primarily because of its mechanistic and scientific claims (and, one may add, pretensions), but because it delves into the mysterious sources of creativity, imagination, and the non-rational, magical factor responsible for the creation of psychic order.

Psychoanalysis studies the jaguar that occupies the other partially sealed-off cell of the mind, the unconscious. Often, too, there is a motive at the outset of analysis to get control of the unconscious. Analysands may initially think that they will be able to put their hands on great powers if they learn the code of the unconscious. This power quest usually ends, however, as it does in the story of Tzinacan, with the realization of the ego's proper position within the larger psychic universe. The ego is not meant to be in charge of the psyche as a whole. This is a spiritual realization in analytic terms. The spirituality that comes about through analysis leans on this realization and the experience of the self. Some clinical examples may serve to illustrate how the spiritual enters in the course of a personal analysis.

A new client brings a first dream to analysis. A particular detail in the dream catches my attention. In the dream, he is having breakfast in a resort hotel room and the window is wide open. Outside he sees the ocean. A moderately strong sea breeze is blowing, and a white curtain billows into the room. I ask him to describe this more carefully.

"It's a mild breeze," he says, "very fresh. Sometimes there is a gust of wind and the curtain, you know, billows", he adds, gesturing widely with his arms. "It's a clear sunny day and the breeze is fairly strong, but not threatening. It's a good day for the beach, or for sailing."

As he tells me this, he falls into a mild state of reverie, and I follow him into this mood. For a moment it seems like we have entered the dream together, and I feel the breeze and taste the salty air. I muse to myself: the window is open, there is access to the unconscious, and the timing is propitious. It's a good moment to begin analysis.

Several weeks later he recounts a second dream. He is standing on the bank of a large river. Around him and in the water he sees many women and children playing, bathing, and generally relaxing. He enters the water and begins swimming, and he notes how clear and clean this river is. He can see the bottom, and he enjoys the refreshing cool feeling of the clean water on his skin. He swims out quite a long distance and is about to round a bend when suddenly he spots a great white shark lying quietly on the bottom of the river some 20 or 30 feet beneath the surface. Frightened by this, he quickly turns back and gets out of the water. He wonders why the women and children do not seem to care and go on swimming and playing around in the water. Don't they see the shark? Or do they know it's not dangerous? Or has he hallucinated the shark and it's not real? He does not understand and wakes up.

The dream is disquieting but not terribly frightening, I think to myself. The shark is quiet right now, but what does its presence out there under the surface mean? Why does the dream-maker show us a shark? Is this a communication to us both to proceed with caution in the analytic exploration of the unconscious? In preceding sessions, he had offered a narrative of his life that gave us some material to associate to this dream image. We both thought of the shark as a reference to a psychotic break he had suffered during a drug trip some 30 years earlier. This was a traumatic experience that deeply marked his life. "I was frozen in the eye of God," he said in this session referring back to the nightmare of the drug experience. "I could see my sin. God was pointing his finger of accusation right at me. I saw so very clearly that I was utterly corrupt and rotten. Everything I had done in my life was bad, bad, bad! I was the greatest sinner in the world! When I realized this, I was all alone and God was looking at me only, and His devastating judgment was absolute and final."

As he thought about the dream, it seemed that the great white shark had once attacked him and devastated his ego. For him this was a spiritual experience of the first order, but one that overwhelmed his ego and left him severely wounded. He was traumatized. "That's why I got out of the river of life," he said. "My life stopped at that moment. I longed to go back to the person I was before the attack, but I couldn't. I was trapped by this knowledge that God had me in his vision and that I was totally bad. And I couldn't figure out why other people weren't equally devastated by this knowledge." It had taken him years to recover his balance.

"The shark is quiet right now," I ventured. Perhaps this would calm his emotions, I thought, and allow us to go on reflecting on the dream as it referred to the present.

"Oh yes, but he can attack at any moment. Those sharks can move like lightning, and when they do it's all over."

"The women and children seem OK," I pointed out.

"Yeah, that's strange. I don't get it." Silence reigned for a time after this exchange.

In Borges' story, Tzinacan is protected from the jaguar by a thick stone wall and a barred window. In my patient's dream, nothing but clean water separates the swimmer from the shark. This is important and indicates different structures and psychic defenses against the terror of a primitive psychic object that can represent the self in its negative aspect as destructive and punishing. Jung refers to this when he writes in *Answer to Job*: "God has a terrible double aspect: a sea of grace is met by a seething lake of fire, and the light of love glows with a fierce dark heat of which it is said 'ardet non lucet' – it burns but gives no light. That is the eternal, as distinct from the temporal, gospel: one can love God but must fear him" (Jung 1954/1969: para. 733). Jung is referring not to God in the theological or metaphysical sense as spoken of by theologians and philosophers, but rather of a God of primary religious experience, an archetypal image. This psychological factor may take the manifest form of a great white fish or a jaguar. The self manifests in dreams and visions as a highly ambiguous image full of inner tensions and contradictions that can be resolved only at the level of the archetype *per se*, which is beyond our knowing, as is Divinity. What we experience is always just a piece of it, never the whole.

Analysis opens the window to powerful psychic figures and forces, which display this kind of power and ambiguity. Spirituality in the context of psychoanalysis is consequently a high-risk venture into the unknown, entering into the waters of the unconscious and opening us to the other side of our walled-in psychic containers. The pioneers – Freud and Jung – knew well the fear of confronting the unconscious and venturing into these uncharted areas of the mind. Freud faced the mortally dangerous sphinx; Jung confronted archetypes of the collective unconscious in their vast variety of forms and spoke of them with fear and trembling. Psychoanalysis is an effort to discern the central mysteries of human existence and to consider its major riddles, if not answer them. This enterprise leads to a kind of spirituality that is grounded in personal experience of the archetypal images of the self.

In another key example, analytic experiences sometimes show the unconscious spirit's freedom and genius for novelty and invention, which is extraordinary and surpasses all conscious expectations. A patient I had been seeing for a little more than a year told me about a dream that totally surprised him. The context of the dream was extraordinary. He told me that he had the dream while sitting on a bench in a hospital waiting for his daughter to have her third baby. He was not happy that their daughter was having this child since she was not well able to support herself and her two children, let alone yet another. So here he was at 2:00 a.m., waiting with his daughter until she would be taken into the delivery room. He fell asleep on the waiting bench and dreamed that he found himself in his daughter's delivery room. Some women are hovering around and tending to things. Suddenly he has a vision (in the dream), and in the vision he sees some 20 people standing around his daughter's bed waiting for the birth. They are here to celebrate this joyful event.

Then he realizes that he recognizes them. Each one is someone he knows from the past. He searches their faces – there is his childhood chum, there is his friend from college, there is his former mentor, and so on and on. He knows them all. In the dream vision, they are the ages they were when he knew them years ago. He is suddenly overcome with joy, for he realizes that some of these people are actually dead now but here they are again! They have come here for him, to be with him at the birth of his new grandchild, and he is filled with immense gratitude that they are here. He weeps for joy to be with his friends again, and at this moment his daughter wakes him up and says it is time for her to go in and give birth.

This dream/vision of a network of relationships, of links between past, present, and future, is akin to Tzinacan's vision of the inter-connectedness of all things and living beings on the high wheel. In such moments we are privileged to transcend our limited ego views and preferences. There are larger realities, temporal and atemporal. The ego's position is relativized. Tzinacan forgot himself; my patient put aside his distress and objection to this birth. A greater perspective takes hold when the self is present in a dream and the ego's position is relativized. This is the spirituality that grows out of the analytic experience.

The type of spirituality that arises in analysis is spontaneous, surprising, and almost always contrary to the ego's limited attitudes and expectations. This is why Jung calls dreams compensatory. They contradict the ego's extreme one-sidedness. The compensating effects of the unconscious may also enter a session in the form of a slip. A client was very carefully telling me about his wonderful new relationship with a nearly perfect woman, but in which now, after three or four weeks, a few minor conflicts and disharmonies were beginning to appear. His girlfriend had a few irritating mannerisms and behavioral quirks that bothered him, but only ever so slightly, he wanted to say. "In no way do I want to say that these things are not important," he emphasized strongly. Then he halted, realizing the double negative had communicated the opposite of what he was consciously intending. Being an experienced psychologist himself, he understood the meaning of slips. When he heard himself voicing his real thought, he began to laugh sheepishly. "You will tell the truth whether you want to or not," I said, laughing with him.

The spirit of the unconscious is truth telling. This guides our work, whether or not the ego finds itself in a cooperative mood. This is another aspect of the spirituality that flows through analytic work.

The psychic energy field that is generated by the relationship between analyst and analysand is another possible entry point into an apprehension of a spiritual dimension. Jung tells of a case of a young woman who idealized him to the high heavens and dreamed of him as Father God carrying her in his arms through a wheat field as the wind swept the grain into waves (Jung

1943/1966: para. 211). The sea wind – pneuma, "spirit" – also blew gently through the open window in my patient's initial dream. I did not mention earlier that I, the analyst, was also a figure in that dream. I was watching the dreamer enjoy a large glass of orange juice and hearty breakfast of eggs and toast. I seemed impatient with him, he said. He wondered if I would end up respecting him or rejecting him. This reminded him of his father and stepfather. In the analytical relationship, a spirit is born that connects the past to the present and may lead to a new future. The bond that develops in analysis is profound and resembles the earliest ties we know, the child-parent relationship but also, and more importantly, it can lead to another type of relationship with the archetypal figures buried within the personal complexes. To fathom and study and fully experience this bond to the archetypal images and powers through the transference is a central work of analysis, and perhaps the heart of the spiritual exercise that psychoanalysis becomes as it deepens in complexity and gathers its full strength. What Jung called "transformation" in analysis has its central energies in the fertile context of this relationship (Jung 1929/1966: para. 160ff.).

Finally, there is synchronicity. Most often this moment of being shown the surprising inter-connectedness of things grows out of a close relationship, sometimes the analytic relationship and sometimes another. The client who slipped and told the truth in spite of himself related, in the same session, an unusual happening. He was not at all given to mystical notions and strove to be a rational, sceptical, modern man in all ways. So he was nonplussed by an incident that took place the day before our session. His daughter had called recently and told him about a nearly fatal accident she had been in while driving an old rented car on a narrow mountain road. A tire blew out on her vehicle and nearly caused her to swerve off the road and tumble to what would have certainly been her death in the deep ravine below. She was quite shaken up, but OK, she told him. The client was telling his son about this incident as they were driving in his car. Just as he was telling him about the blowout on his daughter's car, one of the tires on his own car blew out with a terrific noise and with such force that the rim of the wheel instantly began grinding along the pavement. He was speechless with astonishment at this striking coincidence and felt it was somehow revelatory of the profound links in his family network. The experience added a transcendent dimension to what we had already discovered about the unconscious in analysis. This invisible network of relations, which includes both the psychological and physical aspects of our lives, shows its presence in such moments. If we could see the full extent of it, we would see what Tzinacan saw when he looked up and glimpsed the high wheel. We are each threads in a vast fabric whose extent and design are beyond our comprehension, and we touch each other in strange ways and surprising places.

To summarize spirituality within the psychoanalytic context, I refer to Isaiah Berlin's famous distinction between two types of liberty: positive liberty and negative liberty. Positive liberty, he says, is "freedom for", and entails the use of freedom to instruct, shape, form and reform. It is active. Like the freedom of parents to shape and influence their children, of kings and queens and governors to "improve the common folk", positive liberty is used to impose structures from above downwards. Berlin noted some of the dangers in positive liberty when applied to society and culture. Those who enjoy this type of freedom tend to take it upon themselves to instruct others how to live the good life based upon their own certainties about what constitutes self-actualization, growth, and enhanced living. They are the heirs of Rousseau and Romanticism, and they turn out to have been some of the worst tyrants, dictators, and fascists of modern times. All were intent upon improving society, even the human race, but their certainties and their strong exercise of power turned ugly and lethal for people who did not fit their paradigms. Negative liberty, on the other hand, is "freedom from" and protects the individual from external compulsion, from authoritarian (even if well-intended) thought and behavior police. It is the condition of being able to do what you want to do, when and how you want to do it. It is freedom from tyranny and is passive rather than active. Berlin recognized the dangers of this kind of liberty as well, since it can lead to individualism and self-indulgence, but he favored it because on the whole, he felt, people can figure out for themselves what is best for them and muddle through.

Applied to spirituality, the equivalent to positive liberty is the type of spirituality that is taught in spiritual traditions, which is grounded therefore in the certainties of dogma and traditional practices. Spiritual life in this form has a prescribed course and can be taught in detail. All who follow the ways of it share a common set of images and experiences, although they may pursue positive spirituality with varying degrees of intensity. At its extreme, it can lead to fundamentalist excess, even the self-destruction of martyrdom and terrorism. The form of spirituality corresponding to negative liberty, on the contrary, is empty of prescribed content and relies on an attitude of openness to the unknown. It is an individual spirituality. It is based on an attitude that the Chinese have called *wu-wei*, i.e. letting things happen and unfold on their own. It is therefore passive rather than active. Freud's method of free association and his recommendation to analysts to cultivate neutrality and evenly hovering attention toward their patients' psychic material open the mind to this type of spirituality, as does Jung's practice of active imagination.

There are forms of psychotherapy today that use traditional forms of positive spirituality in their methodologies. If traditional spirituality is combined with a cognitive behavioral approach to psychotherapy, the result is programmatic rather than exploratory, intent on planned objectives rather than open to surprise and individual difference, more proactive than reflective. Psychoanalysis tends strongly to take the other way of open spirituality, recognizing that the spirit bloweth where it listeth and that humans cannot foresee its directions or control its ways. The spirit of the unconscious must reveal itself ever anew, ever fresh.

Both forms of spirituality have their values and strengths as well as their weaknesses. It is also possible to combine them in a type of practice that might use traditional forms to begin with but allow for openness to new directions as the process goes on. Within the context of Jungian psychoanalysis, however, the bias is strongly in favor of openness and opposed to prescriptions and recipes.

Psychoanalysis, as a method of investigation, discovery and healing, studies the patterns on the jaguar's back when the light shines into the temenos that is our analytic cell. It is a practice of open-ended spirituality that observes the irrational and attends to the surprising hidden linkages that infiltrate our lives and connect us to all that exists. Analysis is a sustained reflection on the God's script, which becomes manifest as we mind the self. Consciousness of the message inscribed in our souls heals our one-sidedness and neurotic illnesses. The net effect is immense gratitude.

Chapter 10

Mapping the psyche

As exciting as exploration of the unconscious can be, it must be recognized that after intense scrutiny of the psyche's images and energies one may be left with a *massa confusa*, that is, a collection of images and memories that have great potential for new life and revelation but no discernable shape or pattern. Thus the need arises to find the architectural framework that can contain these experiences and show their relationship to one another and to one's own self-conscious awareness. I think we can assert without too much hesitation that a primary and universal function of the human mind is to create order. Sometimes it may be a matter of discovering order that already exists but is faint or invisible at first glance. At other times, it becomes a matter of imposing order by sorting and filing.

Map-making is a function of this need and the resulting cognitive activities that follow. It seems that maps of an ordered cosmos are found in cultures of all types and times. A sense of order seems to be needed at a deep and universal human level. Levi-Strauss states this point with wit and elegance: "This necessity for order is at the foundation of the thought that we call primitive, but only inasmuch as it is at the foundation of all thought" (Dubuisson 2007: 19). Insofar as humans are thinking creatures, they seek order. Hence the universality of maps.

The need for establishing a sense of order becomes especially apparent during times of stress and internal chaos. Then the mind gets busy and searches out ways to find, even to impose, a sense of order. This can be a defense against impending chaos or simply a way of coping with confusion. Some people are better at map-making than others, and some seem to have a much higher need for order than others. But in times of major crisis, whether personal or collective, a map can be exceedingly useful for orientation and containment. Such a critical situation confronted Jung, beginning around the end of 1912 and extending until around 1918. During this period of internal upheaval and emotional turmoil, he created his most important personal mandalas and also the theory of the psychological types, both of them serving as ordering instruments for the psyche. They are maps of the psyche, partially personal to him but also with application to others.

A map is a depiction of order in a specified domain – geographical (land masses), astronomical (stars and planets), spiritual (invisible worlds) or mental (psychic objects such as complexes, archetypes, etc.). A map of the known elements within a given terrain also depicts the relationship among the various objects to one another within that domain. Each individual object is thus contained within a larger structure and has a relationship to all the other objects in that domain. Maps show contexts that hold and contain specific items. In a sense, what Tzinacan discovered in his vision of the great wheel was a map of the spiritual world.

Maps provide, in addition to a sense of order, two essential elements that assist with conscious functioning: orientation and containment. All of these functions are important for survival, whether this be physically, emotionally or spiritually.

There are of course many kinds of map. One of them is cosmographic. Cosmography is the science of mapping the whole universe. Cosmologists speculate and theorize about the beginnings of the universe; cosmographers map the universe. Ancient cosmographers created a high order type of map that depicted the entire known, perceived and believed-in structure of reality. Cosmographical maps appear throughout recorded history and show the relationship among such elements as earth, stars and planets as well as humans and gods and other spiritual entities. Typically they show mankind's place within an ordered framework of the cosmos. Traditional cosmographical maps were made up of combinations of astronomy, astrology, geography, anthropology, and theology. They reflect the structuring activity of the mind as it seeks to find order in the universe and to locate the human within a larger picture of the cosmos. As the scholar of religions, Daniel Dubuisson, defines cosmographical maps, they are "'systems,' 'productions', or 'creations' to designate … universes conceived of by human beings wholly in order to inscribe their persons and existence therein and thereby give them meaning" (Dubuisson 2007: 216, n.8).

Human consciousness has progressed through many versions of cosmographical structure. In ancient times and throughout the Middle Ages, the place of humans was fixed imaginatively more or less in the center of the cosmos, between the realm of Deity above and the realm of animals, plants and minerals below. This organization resulted in what came to be known as "the great chain of being", which was assumed in many writings well into the Renaissance. In the arrangement depicted on such cosmographic maps, the hierarchical order between various levels of being was clearly established. Humans could find their place, and in this way also discover their relation to a whole range of beings such as gods, angels, animals, men, women, rulers, ruled, and so forth. There were obvious social and political assumptions embedded in such depictions of an orderly world.

When we come to Jung's time, that is, the late nineteenth and early twentieth centuries, we confront an entirely new understanding of the cosmos, the earth's and humanity's place in the universe, and the history of the physical universe. Geology had transformed the understanding of the planet's history, replacing the biblical version of creation; biology and evolutionary science had radically altered perceptions of where humans belong in "the chain of being"; and psychology and psychoanalysis were re-mapping the interior world of the human psyche and displacing the conscious ego from the central position as the earth had been replaced by the sun as the center of the solar system. Cosmology had completely changed since the pre-Enlightenment era, and cosmography had followed suit. Maps of the universe no longer included spiritual beings. Positivist science now controlled perceptions of reality, and theology and mythology were excluded from consideration.

Now the inner world of the psyche needed a map of its own, since its contents were no longer being projected into the physical universe. The figures of mythology would have to find a place in the psychic universe, not in the cosmographical rendition of the physical universe. We can call these psychographical maps, corresponding to the cosmographical ones that depict the physical universe. Inner and outer had been sundered, and this required two different types of map. For himself and ultimately for psychology, Jung made several maps of the interior world of the psyche. His maps follow the discoveries of depth psychologists as the maps of the cosmographers follow the discoveries of cosmologists.

Like cosmographic maps, psychographic maps show the relation of individual objects to one another and depict a "whole", which in this case is a picture of the inner world of the psyche. They also offer the user of them a sense of orientation and containment. Jung's psychographic maps bring together into an orderly framework his discoveries of the contents of the inner world and show their relationships to one another. In the creation of these psychographic maps, we see his ordering mind at work, creating a system of psychic object relations by arranging the images of inner experience into a coherent pattern.

We know from *Memories, Dreams, Reflections* and from *The Red Book* that Jung was plunged into a state of disorientation and inner confusion during and after his break with Freud and the Freudian movement in 1912-13. At a certain moment, he decided to follow what he called "the Spirit of the Depths", and with that he set out to discover an unknown realm of inner images, threatening forces, instructive figures and dark shadows. Using his powers of introspection, his intelligence, and the tool he developed for this exploration, "active imagination", he attempted to find his way through a maze.

The results are brilliantly recorded and worked out in *The Red Book*. The basic contents that form the bedrock narrative of *The Red Book* were recorded between November 1913 and June 1916. The paintings were entered into its pages between 1915 and 1929. Throughout this period, Jung was also working on the secondary level of the text where he added his reflections, interpretations and other additions to the primary material. Writing out the text in calligraphic script, he constructed the work that he titled *Liber Novus*.

From the published record, we know that in the early phases of this period a great wave of material flooded into Jung's consciousness in the form of visions, dreams, and active imaginations. After that, he went to work on this material – reflecting, interpreting, painting, and putting into order what he had experienced. A result of this ordering process was the now famous mandala entitled *Systema munditotius*, painted sometime in early 1916 (Figure 10.1).

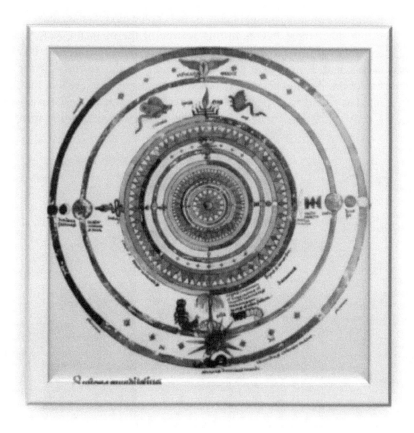

Figure 10.1 Jung's *Systema munditotius*.

In this colorful and balanced mandala, Jung shows us his initial psycho-graphic map. It is a carefully-constructed depiction of the contents of the inner world that he had discovered in the previous two years, and it shows the relation of the parts to one another and to the whole. It is Jung's map of the deep psyche as he experienced it at this time in his life, a map of archetypal structures and figures. This is what he says about it some years later: "It shows the polarities of the microcosmos within the macrocosmic world and its polarities" (Jung 2009: 364).

Looking more closely at the details of this psychographic map, we find the following (Figure 10.2).

At the top, we find a group of four figures: 1) Erikapaios or Phanes (the boy, in a winged egg); 2) a candelabra with seven flames, beside which stand the words "*ignis*" and "*eros*"; 3) *ars*, a winged serpent or worm; and 4) *scientia,* humorously shown as a winged mouse. About Phanes, Jung says: "At the very top, the figure of the young boy in the winged egg, called Erikapaios or Phanes and thus reminiscent as a spiritual figure of the Orphic Gods" (Jung 2009: 364).

About the other three figures in this section of the mandala, Jung writes that there is "a light-tree in the form of a seven-branched candelabra labeled *ignis* ('fire') and *Eros* ('love'). Its light points to the spiritual world of the divine child. Art and science also belong to this spiritual realm, the first represented as a winged serpent and the second as a winged mouse (as a hole-digging activity!) – The candelabra is based on the principle of the spiritual

Figure 10.2 Detail from the top (North) of the *Systema munditotius*.

number three (twice-three flames with one large flame in the middle)" (Jung 2009: 364).

In summary, this section of the mandala contains aspects of the psyche that represent its spiritual nature – high strivings and aspirations, intellectual and meaning-creating functions, the potential for enlightenment. One might refer to this as the higher or upper self.

At the South Pole of the cosmographic map and opposite to the figures at the top in the North, we find a contrasting group (Figure 10.3).

There is a figure named Abraxas, a tree of life, a "monster" (*Ungeheuer*) and a grub (*Engerling*). About this group of figures, Jung writes: "His dark antithesis in the depths is shown here designated as Abraxas. He represents the *dominus mundi*, the lord of the physical world, and is a world-creator of an ambivalent nature. Sprouting from him the tree of life, labeled *vita* ('life') … the lower world of Abraxas is characterized by the number five, the number of the natural man (the twice-five rays of his star). The accompanying animals of the natural world are a devilish monster and a larva. This signifies death and rebirth" (Jung 2009: 364).

This region of the psychographic map represents the natural and material aspect of existence and its cycles of death and rebirth. The ruler of this region

Figure 10.3 Detail from the bottom (South) of the *Systema munditotius*.

of the whole is named Abraxas, and this figure is the counterpart of Erikapaios/ Phanes above. This is the lower self: the somatic and instinctual part of the psyche, not heaven-bound or upward-striving but earthy and rooted in material existence.

The vertical axis of the psychographic map represents the tension between the spiritual and the instinctual poles of the psyche.

The horizontal axis represents the other chief polarity in the psyche – West v. East. On the left or West side of the map, we find several figures arranged in what looks like a set of planetary orbits (Figure 10.4).

About this region of the psychographic map, Jung comments: "To the left we see a circle indicating the body or the blood, and from it rears the serpent, which winds itself around the phallus, as the generative principle. The serpent is dark and light, signifying the dark realm of the earth, the moon and the void (therefore called Satanas)" (Jung 2009: 364). This part of the map represents the phallic, or masculine, aspect of the psyche. It is morally ambiguous (both black and white and named "Satanas") but creative, and it tends toward the dark lower region of the mandala, the earthy and the instinctual. The left side draws the psyche downward toward the instinctual roots of life, so toward sexual enactment and engagement with the material world.

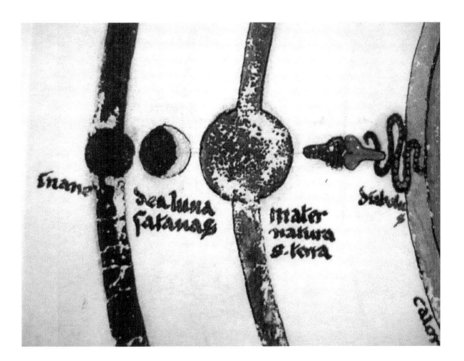

Figure 10.4 Detail from the left (West) of the *Systema munditotius*.

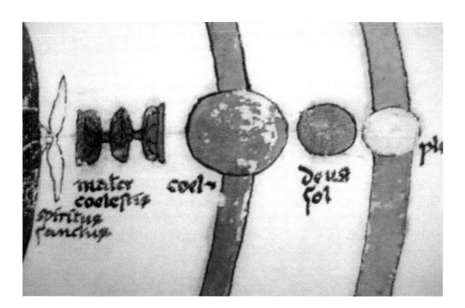

Figure 10.5 Detail from the right (East) of the *Systema munditotius*.

While West pulls toward South, in the East there is the counter-movement toward the North (Figure 10.5).

In the East one finds images of a dove, a chalice, the heavens and the sun, moving outward toward "fullness". Of this side, Jung writes: "The light realm of rich fullness lies to the right, where from the bright circle *frigus sive amor dei* [cold or the love of God] the dove of the Holy Ghost takes wing, and wisdom arises and wisdom (Sophia) pours from a double beaker to left and right. – This feminine sphere is that of heaven" (Jung 2009: 364).

The right side of the map shows affinity with the higher regions, tending upward toward the light, toward the spiritual realm, which is ruled by Phanes, the contrary of Abraxas below. The right side of the psychographic map is designated feminine as opposed to the masculine and phallic nature of the left side. As Philemon teaches in the *Septem Sermones ad Mortuous*, which coincides in time with the making of this mandala, the feminine expression of sexuality is spiritual, while the masculine expression is earthy and instinctual (Jung 1963b: 387). The horizontal axis of the map expresses the tension between the instinctual and the spiritual in sexual terms: the one tends/thrusts downward and creates physically and materially, the other pushes upward toward spirit and archetype and contains.

In the mandala, *Systema munditotius*, Jung is sorting and arranging the energies and tendencies represented by the various figures he has confronted in his active imaginations and recorded in *Liber Novus* – for example, Elijah (*logos*) and Salome (*eros*), the bird-soul and the serpent-soul, Ammonius (the spiritual hermit) and the Red One (the pleasure-seeker).

In the center of the mandala lies a group of descending concentric circles that surround a small orb (Figure 10.6).

Jung writes of this: "The greater circle, which is characterized by points or beams, presents an inner sun within this sphere where the macrocosm is repeated, so that above and below mirror one another. These repetitions are infinite, to be thought of as ever smaller, until the innermost center is reached, the true microcosm" (Jung 2009, 364). The mandala states, therefore, that the microcosmos and the macrocosmos mirror each other – as above so below, as within so without. The *Systema munditotius* indicates an early attempt on Jung's part to chart the relations among a) the individual and personal, b) the collective and archetypal, and c) the impersonal and non-human dimensions of reality and to link individual consciousness thereby to the ultimate structures of reality.

Figure 10.6 Detail from the center of the *Systema munditotius*.

The *Systema munditotius* of 1916 formed a ground-plan for Jung's later thinking and theorizing about the psyche, and it also was the first of further mandalas that he would paint into *Liber Novus* in the years following.

Jung's map-making of the psyche did not cease with these mandalas from *The Red Book* period (1913-1930), however. As I argued in my book, *Jung's Map of the Soul*, his whole psychological theory is an expression of his mind's ordering and mapping tendencies. In the late 1940s, he was again busy with diagrams to describe his conceptualization of the psyche. Ostensibly, these were derived from his studies of Gnosticism (Jung 1950/1968, paras. 347ff.), but we can see clearly that they have strong connections to his psychographic map from *The Red Book* period (Figure 10.7).

In "The Moses Quaternio" (Jung 1950/1968, para. 359), for example, the Higher Adam at the apex of the double pyramid corresponds to Erikapaios/Phanes from the *Systema*, while the Lower Adam corresponds to Abraxas in the lower level of the *Systema*. The inner axes of the horizontal dimension show the same tension between masculine and feminine that we see in *Systema*, with the further complication, however, that there are four figures now instead of only two, made up of two pairs, one a father-daughter couple and the other a brother-sister pair.

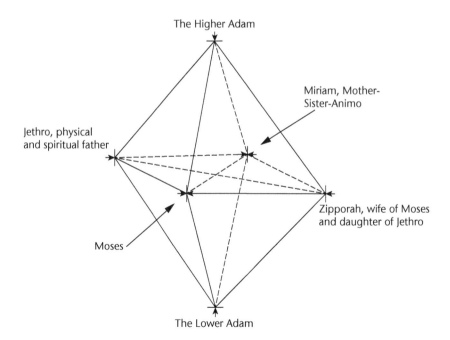

Figure 10.7 The Moses Quaternio.

Descending downward from The Moses Quaternio (re-named the Anthropos Quaternio) (Jung 1950/1968, 231), there are structures that reveal the unconscious and sub-regions of the human self: The Shadow Quaternio, The Paradise Quaternio (Jung 1950/1968, para. 374), and The Lapis Quaternio (Jung 1950/1968, para. 377) (Figure 10.8).

He then stacks them, one on top of the other (Jung 1950/1968, para. 390). In the two Quaternios above the line that he draws through the middle of stack, Homo is at the center and above this is the higher spiritual realm with "Anthropos" at the peak. Below the line lie the material regions (the realm of Abraxas in *Systema*). The two Quaternios below the line ("Paradise" and "Lapis") extend the vertical axis downward into the vegetative dimension of the material world and include the essential components of matter itself (in the Lapis Quaternio), until the diagram reaches all the way through into the subatomic world and dissolves into pure energy. In this map we see Jung's extension of the earlier mandala into territories not explored in *The Red Book* period, which he took up later in his study of alchemy and modern physics. His extensive study of alchemy in the years following *The Red Book* period can be understood, in this respect, as an exploration of the world of Abraxas, the world of materiality and its ruling spirit, Mercurius.

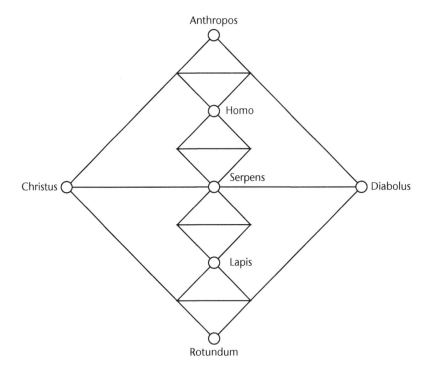

Figure 10.8 Four Quaternities.

What can we take away with us from all of this map-making on Jung's part? Maps serve practical purposes – guidance, orientation, containment. The *Systema munditotius* and later mandalas and psychographic maps provided Jung with a means to orient himself within a vast array of observations and experiences and to direct his thinking along definite lines that eventually resulted in the fundamental concepts of analytical psychology. This was of great value to him during his midlife period, but also later in his psychological theorizing. The maps provided models to assist his hypothesizing. They also played a role in his thinking about psychotherapy, in that the mandala presents a picture of opposites held in tension without splitting, repression, projection, or other defensive operations. For wholeness sake, all aspects of the mandala must be lived consciously. This prevents the one-sidedness that results in neurotic conflict – too much spirituality and not enough instinct, for instance, or the opposite. The maps reinforced the process of individuation by giving visibility to the entire psyche. They therefore further the possibility of gaining and maintaining conscious wholeness despite the pressures from within and without to disown parts of the self for the sake of adaptation and adjustment to social and narcissistic pressures. The psychographic maps portray and encourage the development toward conscious wholeness and are therefore of therapeutic value. They may help practicing psychotherapists to orient their thinking and approach to wholeness rather than partial solutions to immediate problems only. In summary, they are a resource for minding the self.

Chapter 11

Initiation into the Spirit of the Depths

Does it still make sense today to talk about initiation into a type of life that one can call spiritual? Perhaps one can, if a clear distinction is drawn between being religious in a conventional sense and having a spiritual attitude. Throughout modernity, thinkers have speculated that humans were growing out of their need for religion, and by this they often meant not only getting over the childish need for a parental institutional religion but outgrowing, as well, the wish for magical answers and solutions to the riddles of life, in other words "spirituality" in general. References to transcendent realities or spiritual experiences became highly suspect as modern consciousness took hold of cultures and societies. Modernity began with the Protestant Reformation, which rejected the security offered by a Catholic Church and its priesthood, and it culminated during the Enlightenment with its deification of Reason in the French Revolution and the total rejection of religious belief as valid knowledge. As the rational and scientific worldview gained strength in European culture, many intellectuals concluded that the importance of religious faith, even for the masses, would fade away and finally disappear altogether. Science would eventually explain, concretely and materially, what religions had sought to account for with their mythologies and theologies, and what science could not explain at the present time would be left for further research or would be declared nonsensical speculation without merit or possible answer. What Aristotle referred to as "something within ... that is divine" would in time be discovered in a set of neurons that can be measured and photographed or would evaporate with all other mythological thinking. Scientific logic would ease myth out of the picture entirely. The need for myth would dry up, and humans would be free to live a purely rational and sensible life without reference to anything beyond the material world as science knows it and consumerism celebrates it.

Social scientists, historians and philosophers adopted this line of thought as well. Modernity has finally created an irreversible and highly defensible type of consciousness that no longer depends on or needs myth and symbol. Modern consciousness does not orient itself toward or by images of transcendent

Being, but only by practical, rational and instrumental notions derived from its own assumptions about the material basis of reality. Psychology and the other social sciences have effectively interpreted and rationally understood all myth and theology, and thus have emptied them of symbolic value. They have replaced mythic story with scientific knowledge. If a sense of greater meaning for life necessarily requires myth and symbol, then humans must mourn the loss and move on to live without meaning. Soon it will transpire that the longing for spiritual vision and transcendent meaning will disappear altogether from humanity and be replaced by the joys distributed by the entertainment industry and the enticements of technological and pharmaceutical stimulation. People will just forget about spirituality, and so initiation into the spiritual will become a relic of the past, maybe practiced with tongue in cheek in Masonic lodges and private clubs but not taken seriously by the secular world. Or, if a spiritual experience does happen by accident, it will be considered regressive, a throwback to earlier states of consciousness in childhood or when the symbolic spoke to people, or diagnosed as pathological. For those who have advanced to the state of modern consciousness, initiation into the spiritual is now regarded as a mere relic of outmoded, pre-modern attitudes, or perhaps as a sign of false consciousness, a fake, or as mischievous play-acting.

If this is true, it would clearly mean that the archetypal psyche has been totally sublimated by the rational mind and that what remains of myth and symbol in the contemporary world is nothing but a literary memory of what has been and is no more. Free of the gravitas of myth and symbol, the modern person can lighten up and play with the stories and images of antiquity as told in what were once considered sacred texts, which, however, have no convincing resonance any longer with the depths of the present psyche. We are left with collective memories but without soul. The basis of culture has shifted from the spiritual to the material. One must adjust or be marginalized.

It is curious that this was already the state of mind reflected in Jung's account of his personal crisis in 1913. It was this perception about the soulless condition of modernity that pushed him to leave the Spirit of the Times and follow the Spirit of the Depths. The result was *Liber Novus* (*The Red Book*). Not only Jung, however, but also recent sociologists like Peter Berger and theologians like Harvey Cox have registered that questions of transcendent meaning and various offers to answer them continue to appear, but these come from surprising sources like the "secular city". These modern and post-modern resources do not announce themselves explicitly as symbolic, however. The archetypal dimension returns instead in new and hard-to-decipher signals. Jung speculated, for instance, that the worldwide appearance of flying saucers in the 1950s was the signal of a new myth in the making and therefore of an emergent and modern expression of transcendence (Jung 1958/1964a).

Initiation into the spiritual continues today, moreover, and in earnest at the psychological level despite the severe inhibitions imposed by modernity. The difference is that this is not necessarily interpreted as a breakthrough of the supernatural. It is taken up by the modern person and read to mean an opportunity for psychological development and a thrust forward in the movement toward greater consciousness. In this shift, the supernatural has been sublimated by modern thought into the psychological. Gnosis becomes a psychological state of inner conviction and insight that does not depend upon the supernatural warrants of authenticity. The spontaneous arrival of gnosis is not taken to be absolute knowledge about the nature of reality. Rather, it is self-knowledge, a sense of conviction, the harbinger of a new and greater psychological identity. Nor is it necessarily coincident with an obvious state of need or discomfort that calls out desperately for an answer to the question of life's ultimate meaning. Without conscious need or provocation, the psyche may offer gnosis spontaneously. In this case, it may answer a question that has been held unconscious by cultural repression. Modern thinkers may be correct when they claim that people nowadays simply do not experience the need to ask the meaning question, but even they may be taken by surprise and experience transcendence spontaneously, as in Mark Strand's poem, "My Name" (Strand 2005), thereby receiving the shock of an unconsciously-motivated initiation into the spiritual.

Reading Mark Strand's poem, I was reminded of an experience I had when I was struggling with vocational questions in my youth. I had just put my head down one afternoon to take a nap when I distinctly heard my name called softly. I sat up immediately to look for the speaker, but no one was there. This gave me a very peculiar feeling. Strand captures the shiver of astonishment one feels when the natural and familiar world that seems to be running along quite smoothly on a known track of consciousness is suddenly interrupted: "… I felt for an instant/ that the vast star-clustered sky was mine, and I heard/ my name as if for the first time…" (Strand 2005). One's name is called "faint and far off", as he says, by a voice that belongs to "the silence". These lines offer a poetic account of a spontaneously-induced initiation into spiritual awareness. Today, experiences such as this are often misunderstood or pathologized.

Modernity does not show much acceptance of spiritual utterances from the Beyond. Depth psychology understands them, however, as messages from the unconscious, which can have great significance in a person's life. They may signal an initiation into the Spirit of the Depths and lead to a vocation, whose key feature is being personally addressed by the archetypal self. One's name is called by a voice that emanates from the center of the mandala.

Within the religious traditions, such experiences of being addressed by Divinity are familiar. The Bible, for instance, is replete with them – Moses addressed by Yahweh at the burning bush on Mount Sinai; Jacob confronting and wrestling through the night with the Angel of the Lord; the boy Samuel hearing his name called three times in the night; the invisible voice from heaven speaking as Jesus is baptized by John in the River Jordan. Whether a spontaneous initiation into the spiritual extends beyond this singular moment and results in a radical transformation of identity and a new sense of vocation depends on the subject's receptivity to the message and on further events that follow. The biblical personalities do show a dramatic change in identity as a result of their initiatory experiences: Jacob receives a new name, Israel, from the mysterious opponent in the night and goes forward with a destiny to found an eponymous people; the timid Moses accepts his divine commission from Yahweh and becomes the bold leader of the Hebrews as they journey toward the Promised Land; Samuel becomes a prophet of Israel; Jesus enters his ministry with a mission based on his felt identity with the Father.

Initiations by the spirit introduce and induce people into a new kind of consciousness that answers questions related to a sense of identity and consequently lead to meaningful action. In contrast to initiations that are sponsored by and dedicated to the social world – baptisms, bar mitzvahs, weddings, etc. – which answer questions about who one is with respect to one's community and one's social location, initiations into the spiritual world tell of why one was born and of a destiny for one's unique life. The questions answered here are not "Who am I?" or "What is my name?" or "Where do I stand in relation to other people?" They are rather: "What is the meaning of my life from the perspective of Divinity?" "What is my destiny?" The result of receiving an initiation in the spiritual vertex is a sense of transcendence and "gnosis", which is a type of knowledge that is rooted in the archetypal world. This is not rational knowledge. It is noetic (from the Greek *nous*), which means that it is derived from what Aristotle called "something within ... that is divine" and that therefore partakes of eternity.

One of the chief discoveries of depth psychology, which is a strange child of modernity, is that archetypal images, ideas and processes may manifest whenever and wherever they will, spontaneously, unwilled, and unsolicited. They are an indelible feature of conscious existence, woven into the fabric of human life. They cannot be removed by cultural bias or prejudice, only perhaps repressed partially and for a limited time. There is nothing in this that requires belief in a supernatural order. Writing with cautious scientific modesty, Jung aligns himself with such modern thinkers as Adolf Bastian, Hubert and Maus, Emile Durkheim and others when he says: "If I have any share in these discoveries [of 'unconscious thinking'], it consists in my having shown that archetypes are not disseminated only by tradition, language, and migration, but that they can rearise spontaneously, at any time, at any place, and without any outside influence" (Jung 1938/1954, para. 153).

In fact, he demonstrated at length and in detail the archetypal processes that lead to spiritual development in the modern person who is not contained within any religious traditions, and this he named the individuation process. In extensive commentaries on the dreams and visions of several notable people in analysis with himself and others, he lays this development out in graphic detail, step by step. These case histories, moreover, show numerous initiations into the territory covered by the term "spiritual", though with little reference to anything supernatural. The point is that these people were modern by any standard, and yet they received psychological gnosis in great depth and abundance. In Jung's view, the reality of the psyche does not become subsumed under or sublimated by the attitudes and postures of collective consciousness, be they modern or otherwise conditioned. The psyche remains free to offer its astonishing revelations within the modern cultural context as anywhere else. For the people whose individuation processes were discussed by Jung, analysis provided the occasion for an initiation into the Spirit of the Depths and the setting in which they extended and deepened this initiation into a full spiritual development. Analysis was where they learned to mind the self.

Whether interpreted psychologically or metaphysically, the process that unfolds in individuation shows a progression of levels or stages, not regular and linear but rather abrupt, sharp and definite. The surprising and spontaneous initiation into a further stage of gnosis and into an identity that matches it came, for example, to a modern woman who awoke one morning and found herself with the following memory of a dream:

> I am walking along a long covered walkway that is very "architectural" with high ceilings, tall pillars on my left, and unmarked doors in the wall to my right. It is a monumental space and made entirely of gray stone. There is no one else in sight. The doors are shut and show no indication of what lies beyond. I am looking for the Psychology Institute. This space has an otherworldly feeling to it. I see an open door and walk into a room. People of many nationalities are inside. Some are Chinese. A man dressed in white, who looks like someone I know, says in a matter-of-fact voice: "You are here to find out why you were born." He points to a bed that I am to lie down on and places a clear gel over the surface. I lie down on it and am covered with a blanket. He turns my head slightly to the right and a fluid flows out of my ear. I ask about this, and he says it is the cause of my arthritis. Later we go into a second room, and I sit on a chair. Later still, I am standing in yet another room and people, all of them dressed in white, form a line and stand before me, one by one. I am to look deeply into their eyes and determine where their consciousness resides and who they think they are, then I am to look deeper and deeper until I see their soul. My job

is to connect people to their souls. There is only a brief eye contact. Then they go on. The job is done like this. Now I understand why I have been born – it is to do this work of connecting people to their souls.

This dream, which simply arrived as dreams typically do, unsought and unasked for, follows the classic form of initiations. First, there is a sense of being removed from ordinary social life and entering into a temenos, a sacred and protected space. The monumental architecture implies this. This initial movement sets the stage for a transformational ritual, including a healing ceremony, followed by a period of liminality while the subject sits and waits in an intermediate room. This middle stage of the process is followed by a return to society with a new identity and consciousness of mission, in short, a vocation. At the time of the dream, this woman was living in retirement after a long career as a psychotherapist. It is therefore clear that this dream does not represent an initiation into a social/professional identity, a persona, but rather into the spiritual, which speaks about the deeper meaning of her life's work, a vocation that is not tied to a specific job or profession. At the time of the dream, she was not asking for meaning; meaning simply arrived. As a modern person, she has no affiliation with organized religion, does not believe in Creedal statements about the Divine or the supernatural, and was not in any sort of existential crisis requiring an "answer" of ultimate meaning. Existential anxiety, if such there was, in this case was entirely unconscious to her. She could have said she was done with meaning, but evidently meaning was not done with her. Initiation into the spiritual typically announces itself in the psyche of modern people spontaneously and without conscious request or intentional preparation for it. It comes because it has to happen.

Sometimes it is so shocking and anxiety-provoking that it leads to a request for psychotherapeutic treatment. The all too familiar and by now cliché ridden midlife crisis in modern societies, which can and often does initiate a person into a period of profound psychological transformation, is an example. The crisis can nevertheless offer the opportunity for an initiation into the spiritual if taken up as such. One needs to recognize that the initiation into the spiritual is based on archetypal processes and runs from archetypal energies beyond the reach of ego consciousness, and therefore it does not require social intent or engineering. It need not be explicit or public. In modernity, in fact, this initiation is typically unofficial, undesired, and sometimes seemingly pathological. It often comes in the guise of private suffering such as unaccountable or stubborn depressions, and the process following is played out in the analyst's office. Joseph Henderson documents several instances of this in his classic study, *Thresholds of Initiation* (Henderson 2005).

Above the threshold of the entrance to his house, Jung placed a stone with the Delphic oracle: *Vocatus atque non vocatus deus aderit* (Called or not called, the god (i.e., the Spirit of the Depths) will be there). This serves as a mnemonic tool for keeping awareness that initiation into the Spirit of the Depths can catch moderns by surprise at any time and any place. It is not something we have to go looking for in all corners of the world among exotic pre-modern peoples. "It says: yes, the god will be on the spot, but in what form and to what purpose? I have put the inscription there to remind my patients and myself: *Timor dei initium sapientiae* ['The fear of the lord is the beginning of wisdom']" (Jung 1975: 611).

Chapter 12

Humanity's shadow monster

A glaring anomaly about human beings is that they can seem so spiritually elevated at one moment and so demonically possessed at another. This is as true of individuals as it is of masses and mobs. What gets into us? If archetypal images can elevate us to lofty regions of spirituality, they can also throw us down into the pit of the demonic and destructive. We can see this range of psychic forces represented in the *Systema Munditotius*. Rudolph Otto, too, acknowledges the dark side of the *numinosum* in *The Idea of the Holy*. This is the reason for the "shudder" and "dread" that he found in accounts of religious experience worldwide (Otto 1950: 15-19). Jung, as a psychiatrist, was professionally sensitive to the destructive power of the unconscious and painfully aware of the potential for negative fallout from numinous experience in individual lives and in tightly-knit groups like tribes and nations. Archetypal forces can profoundly disturb consciousness, as important as the experience of them may be for linking the ego to the reality of the self.

In *Memories, Dreams, Reflections*, Jung comments specifically on the distorting effect that numinous ideas and images can have on cognition: "Wherever the psyche is set violently oscillating by a numinous experience, there is a danger that the thread by which one hangs may be torn. Should that happen, one man tumbles into an absolute affirmation, another into an equally absolute negation... The pendulum of the mind oscillates between sense and nonsense, not between right and wrong. The numinosum is dangerous because it lures men to extremes, so that a modest truth is regarded as the truth and a minor mistake is equated with fatal error..." (Jung 1963a: 151). In the same remarkable passage, he reflects on an encounter with Freud during the early years of his career as a psychoanalyst when he observed his mentor in the grip of a powerful defense: "My conversation with Freud had shown me that he feared that the numinous light of his sexual insights might be extinguished by a 'black tide of mud'. Thus a mythological situation had arisen: the struggle between light and darkness. That explains its numinosity, and why Freud immediately fell back on his dogma as a religious means of defense" (Jung 1963a: 151). Jung concludes that the numinosity of sexuality had distorted Freud's normally clear thinking capacities. Numinous contents of the unconscious pull thinking magnetically into an orbit where it becomes merely ingenious rationalization, as brilliant as it may be.

This is what one commonly finds in people who are absolutely convinced of a religious teaching. Filled with spirit and belief, their thinking is distorted by an archetypal presence of massive proportions, though largely unconscious, which lends privileged ideas the force of triumphant, dogmatic certainty and serves as a bulwark against opposing threatening images and ideas that seek to balance or thwart it. You can see this in the fanatic's face. A small step further and one finds the willing martyr, whose conviction and identification with the archetypal idea is so extreme that life itself loses significance. Needless to say, this development in consciousness is the exact contrary of the individuation project, which is to make the numinous contents as conscious as possible, to sublimate and integrate them, and to bring them into relation with other quite different aspects of the self, thereby relativizing them.

Jung applied this same critique to national politics in his 1936 paper on the old Germanic god, Wotan, where he offered a psychological analysis of the distorting power of numinous images in the churned up political and social processes tearing apart the cultural fabric of Germany and central Europe at that time (Jung 1936/1964). In this instance, Jung observed, the psychic force field of the manifestly constellated Wotan mythic image had taken possession of an entire nation and was driving Germany to an (at that time) unknown and irrationally determined end. Contrary to what his critics say, Jung did not invent this mythic manifestation in German culture. It was in all the newspapers, and Wotan was explicitly worshipped in some religious circles in Germany at the time. The convincing power of the archetypal image and presence also shielded people from the awareness of guilt for their criminal behavior. Everything could be justified, no matter how heinous. Archetypal possession of a collective group invests certain ideas and policies with absolute certainty and brooks no doubt of dispute. Contrary thoughts and images are savagely suppressed. This was the case with German collective mentality at the time. There was no space for reflection, for questioning, for serious debate, never mind contrary political and social views. Conviction based on archetypal backing seemingly cuts off circulation to the neo-cortex and fires the emotions. The old reptilian and limbic brains take over and rule. Scapegoats are located and piled upon ferociously, which adds fuel to the fires of destruction.

When the curtain came down on the final scene of the Third Reich and the theater in which it played lay in utter and complete ruins, physically and morally, there remained little appetite for myth and symbol in the land. There had been too much of the numinous in the collective psyche, and it had only contributed to the devastation. Myth and symbol were cancelled as cultural options, and irony and rationality took charge of the culture. While defensive, this also represented a return to sanity. The result, however, has been a resolutely militant modernity that harshly rejects religious imagination, which requires some sort of transcendent reference and relation to the numinous. In this burned-out cultural context, it became almost impossible to look upon the mythic without grave suspicion and bitter memory. Understandable enough. Once badly burned, twice shy. Myth was out.

This wariness about the grand enthusiasms generated by archetypal ideas and images has also introduced an uneasy suspicion of Jung's psychology and classical Jungian perspectives on dream interpretation, the hermeneutical method of amplification and active imagination. These methods evoke too clearly for comfort the taboo energies of myth and symbol. What is lost, obviously, is the realization that the numinous experience offers a hint of transcendence. Lost, too, is the notion that the individual is a soul with potential to come into relation with the spiritual in a wholly natural way that does not need to tip over into madness. In contemporary German art, this has begun to emerge gingerly again in the bold symbolic paintings of Anselm Kiefer, Gerhard Richter and Sigmar Polke and in the films of Wim Wenders, where signals of transcendence blink and shine through the tattered fabrics of contemporary life.

It must be said, however, that when the spiritual history of the West is written in the future, the German Nazi-sponsored holocaust will go down ironically enough as perhaps the major spiritual event of the twentieth century. In the long view of Western spiritual history, it is as defining a moment as the crucifixion. Any future Western theological thinker in the biblical and Judeo-Christian tradition who does not place the holocaust at the center of theological reflection on human and divine natures will be missing the mark. After the holocaust one cannot possibly think clearly or truly about the spiritual condition of the West in modern times without devoting a major portion of reflection to this crucial moment in history. It is an event whose very darkness illuminates the radical (and evil) one-sidedness of conscious development in the West and whose critical mass of intense suffering places the implacable obligation for deep change, for transformation of consciousness, upon everyone.

What happened? How did it come about that something as demonic as the holocaust could take place in a modern context where culture had reached such a seemingly high water mark of development? Like a bolt of dark lightening, the holocaust illuminates an invisible demonic shadow that can arise in spite of intellectual refinement and conscious attainments at the top. In the absence of adequate spiritual and ethical containment, modernity is at risk of toppling into the abyss. It is the fate of one-sidedness. The religious void that had befallen Europe opened a space for elemental evil to find its way into the public mind and to take control. What emerged in the void was different from Jung's diagnosis of the Wotanic, which is relatively mild and short-lived and would blow over or soften with time. Here one caught the effect of what Jung later termed "absolute evil" (Jung 1950/1968: para. 19), something beyond even the fury of Wotan's lust for war.

The Nazi manifestation laid bare a truth about the human vulnerability to possession by psychic forces beyond the control of the religious and moral structures available at the time. For the most part, the Christian churches and Western civilization failed the critical challenge to contain the collective forces of envy, hatred, and desire for revenge. For all its words about love and mercy, the structures of religion failed to dam the flood of evil in the moment of testing. Religious authority and conviction, already much weakened by two centuries of modernity and secularization, largely collapsed in the face of raw power and extreme politics and, as Freud wrote after his flight to England in 1939, "proved to be, as the Bible has it, 'but a broken reed'" (Freud 1939: 93).

Without the containment of religious structures and a strong ethical attitude to stand against the dark collective forces beneath the surface of social convention, the archetypal shadow is set loose in the world without restraint on its greed and lust for domination. Empathy and wisdom fall away and leave a vacuum for their opposites to take the field. This is precisely the attitude imaged as the solitary deity, Yaldabaoth, by the so-called Gnostics of two thousand years ago.

According to the Gnostic writing, 'The Apocryphon of John', Yaldabaoth is ironically the offspring of Sophia, the last in a long line of archons descended from "The Monad", which is "a monarchy with nothing above it.... [the invisible] One who is above [everything, who exists as] incorruption, which is [in the] pure light into which no [eye] can look" (Robinson 1988: 106). As the chain of archons proceeds to unfold and development gets underway, the generations advance by couples, and each couple unites to produce the next rung in the chain of being. Each new generation is produced by a cooperative effort of two archons in the preceding generation. This relational pattern suddenly changes, however, in Sophia's generation when she decides to create on her own without consultation and without a mate. The result of her creative efforts is the monster child, Yaldabaoth. Her reaction to him is reminiscent of Hera's response to her parthenogenetic creations, Hephaistos and Ares:

> And when she saw (the consequences of) her desire, it
> changed into a form of a lion-faced serpent. And its
> eyes were like lightning fires which flash. She cast
> it away from her, outside that place, that no one of

the immortal ones might see it, for she had created
it in ignorance. And she surrounded it with a
luminous cloud, and she placed a throne in the middle
of the cloud that no one might see it except the Holy
Spirit who is called the mother of the living. And
she called his name Yaldabaoth.
This is the first archon who took a great power from his mother.

(Robinson 1988: 110)

Yaldabaoth then empowers himself with strength stolen from his mother, and with this derivative power he gets busy and creates a whole crowd of other lesser beings whose principal duty it is to serve him and do his bidding. In this, he shows the most fundamental trait of his character, the insistent desire for complete power and domination. He wants to be served. When he finishes fashioning 365 minions, he looks around with satisfaction and declares himself to be the only real god. Thus he exalts himself imperially above the lesser powers he has created and also, perhaps in ignorance or perhaps in defiance, denies the powers that precede him: his mother, Sophia, and beyond her the source of her being, of whom he is ignorant, the Monad. Everything begins with him.

Yaldabaoth depicts a radically-isolated consciousness, which through pride and inflation severs its connection from its source. The brilliant Gnostic author of 'The Apocryphon of John' penetrated behind the deceptive mask of this type of grandiose ego self-sufficiency and revealed its narcissistic psychopathy. Beyond that, he elucidates the genesis of this ego state in its pathological rupture from history and community.

Taken on its own terms, the Gnostic critique was a radical revision of religious assumptions that were (and are) accepted commonplaces in the monotheistic religions. Any notions of "other gods" and/or "goddesses" is illusion or, worse still, idolatry punishable by whatever means might be necessary. Pluralism, wholeness, completeness, the fullness of being, God as Mother-Father are fiercely denied. The fullness of Being is split and the pieces arranged in a strict hierarchy of values while difference is demonized. Yaldabaoth stands squarely behind this development into narrow monotheism, according to the Gnostic vision. Borderline splitting and narcissistic self-aggrandizement are the hallmarks of Yaldabaoth.

In Yaldabaoth, the Gnostics identified a type of ego-consciousness that was endemic in their cultures, and today we find the identical pattern in ourselves, in our patients, and in our fellow citizens. Yaldabaoth represents the ground plan of the individualistic, controlling, defensive ego so familiar in contemporary life and politics. What the Gnostics identified and named in Yaldabaoth is still with us, perhaps even more so.

Jung placed himself and his depth psychology directly in line with the tradition of the ancient Gnostics (Jung 1938/1967) and consequently with their severe critique of one-sided egoism and so-called rationality. Having produced an original Gnostic-like text himself in "The Seven Sermons to the Dead" (Jung 1963a), he knew about the Gnostic experience of the unconscious psyche first hand. Analytical psychology, based as it is so strongly on Jung's own inner experiences, follows the Gnostics in seeing through the dominant attitudes of the individual, the society and the age to the deeper spiritual and archetypal layers. In doing so, it relativizes the claims to ultimacy made on behalf of the separated, divided and divisive ego's attitudes.

At the same time, however, Jung's psychological theory and psychotherapy do not demonize the ego as such, which is a natural product of development and forms the central core of a person's identity. Rather, an attempt is made to connect ego-consciousness to its ultimate source and the ground of its own being, namely to the self. Like the Gnostics' challenge to monotheistic religion, in which they revealed the basis of monotheism to be the god Yaldabaoth and therefore a less than ultimate power, Jung challenges the inflated ego that would say, "I am the master of the psyche, the only god within the psychological universe." With the Gnostics, analytical psychology challenges the ego's supremacy by insisting that it is not the ground of its own being, that it owes its existence to another power that is greater. For the Gnostics this was Sophia, the mother of Yaldabaoth, and behind her many more archons and powers and ultimately the Mother-Father Monad, the Pleroma. In Jung's more modern diction, this is equivalent to saying that the ego owes its existence to the psyche ("Sophia"), of which it is a part (merely a complex), and ultimately to the self (the "Monad" or "Pleroma"), which supersedes the ego and even the psyche itself in an even larger framework of totality and wholeness.

It was Jung's psychological genius that detected such profound connections between modern depth psychology and the then still very obscure and disregarded Gnostic movement of the ancient world, to recognize in the Gnostics' nearly impenetrable writings experiences that paralleled his own, and to perceive in their spiritual explorations the equivalent of his research into the depths of the psyche. What Gnostic texts expose and Jung's analytical psychology also affirms is the illusory nature of our usual perceptions regarding ego autonomy, independence and control. The Gospel of Truth, for example, shows the ego's characteristic illusion: it lives in a fog of self-deception about its independence and about its lack of origin or need of anything outside of itself. The text points out the ego's fierce resistance to insight into its deeper dependencies upon extra-ego structures. Like Jung, the author of this text diagnoses the malaise (a "nightmare") of this type of ego existence. In this delusional state, the ego suffers massive anxiety and becomes aggressive; it lives in envy and despair. This text recommends as treatment for this malaise, much like Jung, an experience of a symbol that will connect ego-consciousness to the self.

The Gnostics held that Yaldabaoth was the Lord of this world and dominates the human condition. This gave them, understandably, a reputation for pessimism regarding human possibilities on this planet, which ran contrary to the Christian teachings of salvation and grace. For the Gnostics, Yaldabaoth defines human psychological existence. Humans are of necessity ego-bound in the sense of being required to develop an individual ego, and in the Occident especially this "deficiency" has been deemed a virtue and cultivated like a rare and precious flower. We can well see the Gnostic perception of the human condition as an accurate psychological assessment and critique of commonly experienced human behavior in all times and places, and especially so in the West in our century. The Gnostic explanation for the universal human experience of evil and tragedy is arguably a sound one if one interprets the figure of Yaldabaoth as the shadow of ego development. But does the shadow inevitably rule?

Jung ventures to go beyond this grim analysis of the human condition. There is more to the human personality than the ego and its shadow. Yaldabaoth is an archetype that creates and sustains an inevitable development within human consciousness toward the formation of the focal narcissistic ego, but there is also a piece of the ego in its deepest core that is of the self and reflects the Pleroma. In the metaphorical language of the Gnostics, there is a spark of light in the darkness of matter, a redemptive possibility. *The Apocryphon of John* accounts for the creation of humanity with a complicated story that makes this point. Yaldabaoth creates a primal man, Adam, but according to the text he does not create man in his own image but rather in the image of the Pleromatic One whom he had seen in a revelation:

And the whole aeon of the chief archon
trembled, and foundations of the abyss shook. And of
the waters which are above matter, the underside was
illuminated by the appearance of his image which had
been revealed. And when the authorities and the chief
archon looked, they saw the whole region of the underside
which was illuminated. And through the light they saw the form
of the image in the water.

And he said to the authorities which attend him,
"Come, let us create a man according to the
image of God and according to our likeness, that his
image may become a light for us." And they created
by means of their respective powers in correspondence

with the characteristics which were given. And each
authority supplied a characteristic in the form of
the image which he had seen in its natural (form).
He created a being according to the likeness of the
first, perfect Man. And they said, "Let us call him
Adam, that his name may become a power of light
for us."

(Robinson 1988: p. 113)

At the core of the human ego, according to this text, resides the image of the
Absolute, which Yaldabaoth and his minions relate to for guidance and
energy. The human created in God's image, Adam, does turn out to be a most
magnificent creature, one in fact so superior to Yaldabaoth and his 365
"authorities" that they become wildly jealous of him. The Absolute, called
Mother-Father, gives Adam some protection against the powers of Yaldabaoth,
though he is of course still under the sway of the Lord of this world and eventually, as we know, falls victim to temptation and forgets his divine origin.
Yet this fact of Adam's inherent likeness to and indeed identity with Divinity
remains embedded in ego-consciousness. In Jungian terms, this is the point of
contact between ego and self.

Jung's view of the ego, as he reflects upon it in his late work *Mysterium
Coniunctionis* (Jung 1955/1963: paras. 130-32), is similar to the Gnostic
rendition above. This makes him a guarded optimist about humanity, although
this attitude is severely tempered by a critical awareness of the force and
power of the psychic agency behind ego-illusion and the architect of the
nightmare of ego existence, the shadow. According to the Gnostics, humanity
cannot escape the power and wiles of Yaldabaoth without a convincing
revelation of previous and original oneness and wholeness in the Pleroma.
This knowledge is what the "messenger" brings in Gnosticism, and it is what
symbols of wholeness – the mandala, the alchemical lapis, the mystic Christ
– bring in Jung's experience and in his theory of analytical psychology. Both
Gnosticism and Jung's psychology offer a tempered optimism about human
potential, or, put another way, a hopeful realism. Yaldabaoth cannot be ignored
or overcome, but his power is not ultimately in control of human destiny.

If we ask what can replace the Yaldabaothian ideology of narcissistic ego-
development, we may catch a hint from Gnostic texts, from Jung, and from
modern psychological experience. What all of these propose as an alternative
option is a "myth of connectedness". One can only hope that this will be
supported by at least a trace of evolutionary movement at the genetic level of
our humanity as well.

Human culture stands now at the conclusion of a development that began
aeons ago. Its culmination is represented in contemporary politics, economics,

religion, and in our conscious attitudes. Its crown jewels appear to be enlightened rationality and individualism. The ideas of History and of Progress, which are thematic in Greek and Hebrew thought, have come to mean for many that increasing human control over nature and even over history are inevitable, that bigger is usually better, that ego control is a measure of success, that expansion is always a positive virtue, and that one god is better than many gods. This is the work of Yaldabaoth, the expansive and controlling dominant of consciousness that underlies the narcissistic ego.

The unconscious is calling for change. Modern depth psychology has mounted a powerful critique on the isolated ego. As never before, we can see its relativity and its slender archetypal support. The new dominant arriving is a myth of connectedness to replace the one of separation and control. It is based on a realization of the network of relations that ties all peoples together into one pluralistic unity. It requires almost unimaginable tolerance of differences and acute consciousness of interdependence among all the parts.

Is the contemporary person wise enough to effectively analyze and counteract the archetypal force of Yaldabaoth? Our great advantage is that we have been given a vision of the greater psyche out there beyond the realm of ego and its operations. This greater psyche, we now know, is grounded in the self that reaches out to the infinite and to the ultimate mystery of life and creation.

Chapter 13

The problem of ethics

Can the individuation process be squared with an ethical attitude that requires a person deeply to care for other people, the community and the natural world? Isn't individuation basically a selfish, narcissistic undertaking? Does Yaldabaoth not rule here, at least subtly and most of the time? To counter this opinion, Jung stated repeatedly that individuation does not mean individualism and that individuation leads to greater rather than to lesser involvement and intimacy with others and the world. But the question remains nevertheless, and it bears repeated consideration.

One argument in favor of individuation as, in fact, a type of ethical practice is to say that the integrated and whole individual contributes to the health and wholeness of others, indeed of all humankind and the planet. This is the message of the Chinese Rainmaker story. As we know from many reports from his students, Jung was fond of this story as told by his friend, the German Sinologist Richard Wilhelm. As recounted by Jung, Wilhelm told him that while he was living in the port city of Qingdao, located in the northeastern part of China, there was a long dry spell in the region. The land in the countryside was parched, and the crops were failing. As a consequence, many people were facing starvation. They tried desperately to produce rain by performing all the religious rites they knew: "Catholics made processions, the Protestants made prayers, and the Chinese burned joss-sticks and shot off guns to frighten away the demons of the drought, but with no result. Finally the Chinese said, 'We will fetch the rainmaker'" (Jung 1955/1963: 419, n. 211).

So they sent a message to another part of the country asking for the assistance of a well-known rainmaker. Eventually, a "dried up old man appeared. The only thing he asked for was a quiet little house somewhere, and there he locked himself in for three days. On the fourth day the clouds gathered and there was a great snow-storm at the time of the year when no snow was expected, an unusual amount, and the town was so full of rumors about the wonderful rain-maker that Wilhelm went to ask the man how he did it." When asked, the old man replied: "I come from another country where things are in order. Here they are out of order, they are not as they should be in the ordinance of heaven.

Therefore the whole country is not in Tao, and I also am not in the natural order of things because I am in a disordered country. So I had to wait three days until I was back in Tao and then naturally the rain came" (Jung 1930-1945/1997: 333).

It was that simple. The sage put himself in order, and this brought the surrounding natural world into a similar state of order. In turn, this affected the weather and produced what the community needed in order to survive – rain! The individual creating inner order simultaneously brings the surrounding world politically and physically into harmony.

Underscoring this view of social macrocosm mirroring individual microcosm in Confucian philosophy, Herbert Fingarette, in his work *Confucius – The Secular as Sacred*, quotes from the *Analects* of Confucius: "Shun, the great sage-ruler, 'merely placed himself gravely and reverently with his face due South (the ruler's ritual posture); that was all' (i.e., and the affairs of his reign proceeded without flaw)" (Fingarette 1972: 4). Correct ritual gesture resolves social and political issues. When the ruler acts correctly and shows himself to be in balance and order, the kingdom will prosper. Fingarette writes further: "The magical element always involves great effects produced effortlessly, marvelously, with an irresistible power that is itself intangible, invisible, unmanifest. 'With correct comportment, no commands are necessary, yet affairs proceed.' 'The character of a noble man is like wind, that of ordinary men like grass; when the wind blows the grass must bend.' 'To govern by *te* is to be like the North Polar Star; it remains in place while all the other stars revolve in homage about it'" (Fingarette 1972: 4).

The idea behind Wilhelm's story is that the individual (especially the extraordinary or the enlightened individual) has the capacity to affect society and the physical world (for good or ill) because the individual, society, and the natural world are intimately connected parts of a single reality. Plato also portrayed such a state of harmony pertaining among individuals, society, and cosmos: "An ancient ethical theory like Plato's *Republic* argued that a just person in a just society should be understood as a person with a harmoniously structured psyche located in a harmoniously ordered society which itself was located in a harmoniously ordered cosmos. The idea that harmony went all the way down and all the way up gave a sense of purpose – and thus comfort – to human life" (Lear 2005: 197). The difference is that Wilhelm's story includes a magical element – the individual can bring about harmony in the social and natural order. Magic can be understood as synchronicity rather than as a cause-and-effect relationship, which removes the ego's power claim from the equation. From this we can extract the lesson that a personal individuation process can have a positive effect on the surrounding social and natural world. Individuation could be seen as ethically positive since it contributes to the general well-being. It has social utility and so is sound from a teleological ethical perspective (Frankena 1973: 14).

This view recognizes that individuation does not proceed in isolation from the wider world. It is not a sealed-off and isolated process limited to the individual personality. If an individual human being minds the self at the personal level and finds the way toward inner unity of the psyche's inherent polarities, this will enhance order and wholeness as well in the surrounding social and natural worlds. Conversely, if the individual succumbs to inner disorder and disintegrates at a personal level and remains there, this will have a deleterious effect on the surrounding world.

Therefore, individuation includes ethical implications in the deepest sense, in that this psychological and spiritual development fosters a mirroring development in the wider human community and in the natural world. It is not limited to the individual. Without this deep connection to society and nature, individuation could be seen as simply the pursuit of a person's narrow self-interest and private fulfillment without benefit to, and indeed at the expense of, society and environment. If left there, such narcissistic self-indulgence could be called seriously into question on ethical grounds. One is taking energy and resources from the community and the world and returning nothing of value. In this more relational view of individuation, however, there is no inherent conflict between individuation and ethics. They exist side by side in profound harmony, the one deepening and reinforcing the other.

From teachings and stories such as these we might conclude that the individuation process, which requires living as closely and consciously in relation to the self as possible, coincides seamlessly with proper conduct (moral and ethical behavior) in the deepest sense, and that this harmony between individuation and ethics produces beneficial synchronistic effects on the individual's surrounding worlds of society and nature.

Is this really tenable, though? It depends on the validity of synchronicity, which is at best an irrational happening, and so the relation of individuation to ethics seems rather shaky. If it depends on magic or divine intervention, modernity is not convinced. Can individuation be proven to be beneficial to society and the natural world? Can this proposition be tested? People who struggle with individuation issues in daily life often do not consider or recognize that seamless harmony prevails between their individuation choices and the moral order. If their individuation turns out to be of benefit to others, so much the better, but this does not seem to be written in stone. Indeed, quite often these two concerns seem to diverge radically: individuation demands untested, unconventional and individual choice and responsibility, while morality asks for careful consideration of social rules and customs that are meant to promote the common good. It seems that individuation and morality form an uneasy alliance at best and, more often than not, seem to be in outright conflict with one another. From experience, it must be conceded that no individuation process proceeds very far without breaking free from restrictive collective mores and customs. The social conformist is not an individuating personality.

Putting aside for the moment the notion that individuation synchronistically falls in line with the greater good, two questions will be addressed here. First, does ethical sensitivity hold a strong position in the individuation process or is it more of an obstacle to individuation? Second, does individuation have a role to play in the elaboration and development of ethics and moral thinking?

First of all, it must be recognized that at the more advanced stages of development both individuation and ethical reflection are open and dynamic processes, not static and fixed programs. Individuation unfolds through myriad decisions and reflections over the course of a person's lifetime and is full of ambiguities, false or deceptive pathways, and contradictory tendencies. The ethical life as well is not primarily about following social or religious rules and codes but rather about on-going and open-minded reflection on action from a moral perspective. Both individuation and ethical reflection involve a progressive endeavor to incarnate human potential in a specific time and place. How do the two processes intersect, challenge one other, and possibly enhance each other?

Individuation means becoming conscious of who and what one is and is not. It means recognizing one's unique selfhood in all its complexity, including one's social and cultural indebtedness and, beyond that, the influence of archetypal factors without and within. This amounts to becoming conscious of one's selfhood in the broadest and deepest meaning – grasping the mandala in all its aspects. This is not equivalent simply to affirming one's personal identity narrowly construed and asserting it at all costs. Most of what we are is not unique at all. The individual is largely a conglomerate of genetic inheritance, personal and cultural influences and introjections, and archetypal motifs. The miracle of consciousness within this complexity makes it possible to become aware of it as a mandala, but this does not come about as a once-and-for-all "aha". Rather, the mandala is disclosed unevenly and in random moments of insight throughout life as one gains wider life experience and more consciousness of the self as a whole. Individuation consists of the attempt to grasp in consciousness as much as possible the personality in all of its complexity and lived manifestations. One continues to discover and incarnate new facets of the self as long as one lives.

Individuation is not possible, therefore, without benefit of a wide and varied range of life experiences. This development is not limited to introspection and reflection on life-in-general. It comes about through living a life that draws forth many, if not all, of one's potential capacities as a human being, including shadow tendencies, and then reflecting on these experiences and discovering in them the features that we name as persona, shadow, anima and animus, complex, archetypal patterns and images, and, at the center and embracing the whole, the self. A late kitchen philosopher named Jo Coudert, wittily reversing

Plato's epigram, observed that an unlived life is not worth examining. The individuation process requires both action and reflection.

At every important step of the way, ethical questions press into the field of reflection. Individuation calls for countless decisions large and small, and what decision of any consequence is free of ethical issues and dilemmas? Questions of fairness, justice, sensitivity to others' needs, duty to family and society, professional obligations – all these play across and through almost every major decision one takes. Occasionally the answer to these questions is straightforward and easily discovered by checking a moral code or considering conventional rules governing behavior in a specific society or cultural setting. Since many people have faced similar issues before, a body of reflection and deliberation is available. One can ask the pastor or the rabbi for advice or consult the wisdom of the ages in the library. In many cases, however, the rules either do not apply or do not satisfy the needs of further individuation as these push against the boundaries of the conventional and the approved. The very nature of individuation seems to demand going beyond or outside the moral limits of a specific society. In order to live one's life authentically and fully, one must occasionally strike out on one's own and take personal responsibility for unconventional actions. There is the risk that this will not be understood. Perhaps its justification rests merely on shaky emotional grounds. The pressure for individuation comes from within, and its implacable movement can and often does come into conflict with what the surrounding social milieu advocates or condones. This may be due to a culture's narrowness or disorder, so its rules and customs are themselves immoral from a deeper perspective. In his study of Gandhi, Erik Erikson describes this kind of a problematic as Gandhi faced racial prejudice in England, South Africa and India (Erikson 1969). There comes a moment when an inner voice is not satisfied by conventional answers and demands something other. Individuation will inevitably require actions that society does not condone. It does not come without a price. The difficult question becomes one of discernment: where does this voice come from in the psyche, and what does it intend? Often one cannot know. It is simply given, an irrational demand.

Individuals will reach advanced ethical conclusions long before the collective gets there. This is well known. Community values lag behind, sometimes by decades and generations. Racism and sexism, for example, were (and are still) condoned in many areas of the world, and the individual who questions these, or forms relationships that contradict these social norms, must be prepared to take abusive reactions that are collectively approved and sometimes violently delivered. The enforcers of moral standards are not known for their compassion. At an advanced stage of individuation, the moral compass is not an external one. One cannot simply consult a guidebook or an expert and take their advice. The problem rests directly on the shoulders of the individual.

The individual has to decide "to do or not to do", without backing from society or religion and indeed often in the face of their severe condemnation.

For individuation questions that cannot be answered from outside sources, one generally looks to private conscience for the guidance of a higher law or what Socrates called a daemon. This may offer guidance and perspective. Even conscience, however, is often of little assistance in specific cases. If one looks to dreams for guidance from the unconscious, these must be interpreted. Or the daemon may be silent, and its silence requires interpretation. One can be forgiven for shrinking back and refusing to take a decision indefinitely. The moral imperative may cry out for an answer, but one cannot reconcile the warring opposites within. One voice says "Yea", the other "Nay", and the result is a stalemate. This is the critical moment that Jung addresses several times in his late essay, 'A Psychological View of Conscience' (Jung 1958/1964b). He speaks of a "conflict of duties", when one option cancels out the other and both sides claim the favor of Kant's Categorical Imperative, which states: "I must never act except in such a way that I can also will that my maxim should become a universal law" (Kenny 1994: 191). One faces two opposed sets of duty, perhaps the one directed toward further individuation of the self and the other toward the benefit of society or community.

While one result of this dilemma may be stalemate and stagnation, a more insidious possibility can emerge in the form of subtle possession by an archetypal idea or image, which promises a way forward, a "higher road", a "destiny", and a guarantee of absolute knowledge. At first, this might look like a perfect answer to the problem of insoluble conflict: one hears the *vox Dei*, an elevated form of conscience that offers assurance and self-confidence. One begins to feel that a higher power is taking the lead and directing one's decisions infallibly. Generally, this conviction induces a titanic inflation and leads to deaf disregard for other opinions and views. Others are either for or against the directives of such visionary absolute knowledge, and the world is divided into friends and foes with nothing in between. In his essay, Jung aptly calls this "wrong" conscience: "besides the 'right' kind of conscience there is a 'wrong' one, which exaggerates, perverts, and twists evil into good and good into evil … and it does so with the same compulsiveness and with the same emotional consequences as the 'right' kind of conscience" (Jung 1958/1964b: para. 835). Madmen and tyrants are totally convinced in the rightness of their actions because they are possessed by an archetypal image or idea and therefore enjoy a divine mandate to do as they please. A "wrong conscience" can back destructive deeds, offering an indisputable conviction in the correctness, rightness, and justice of the mission.

On the individual level, wrong conscience insinuates itself with special force in times of crisis, when people attempt to take seriously their deepest psychological needs. It colludes with the common and understandable need to defend oneself from criticism when the going gets rough. When individuation breaks out of conventional paradigms, the insufficiently-structured ego personality runs the risk of falling into a state of possession by an archetypal figure or idea that instills absolute certainty on its behalf. This offers an unanswerable rationale against the opposition, whether inner or outer, to the decisions taken, and it silences the guilt that inevitably threatens when one violates social mores and conventional values. Conscience becomes inverted and then arrogantly dismisses the customs of society as inferior to one's much higher viewpoint. Swallowed up by titanic inflation, one feels freed of all external rules and moral codes, superior to them, beyond their reach, a Nietzschean Superman who has ascended "beyond good and evil". Here a degraded variety of ethical reflection, sponsored by wrong conscience, is engendered and begins to speak, in the name of the daemonic vision, for an "ethical view" that supports the inflated ego. Yaldabaoth is in charge here.

At this point, the sense of ethics becomes untethered and loses its relation to Tao. It drives its adherents on a fast lane into a moral desert. Psychologically, ethics has now been taken hostage by an archetypal possession and has become a voice for the demonic god in charge of this realm. Now it seems to be one's ethical duty to follow this god's injunctions to the bitter end and at any cost. Whether instilled by mimicking a demonic social order or by individual identification with an archetypal image or idea, this amounts to a state of bondage in which the ego no longer has access to the self, which is an all-encompassing mandala, a *coincidentia oppositorum*.

The psychological answer to this state of inflation is – further individuation. Individuation calls for separation, for taking distance from all identities and identifications, be they ever so numinous and convincing. This is an ethical move *par excellence*. Ethics is at this point woven into the very fabric of individuation, not something external to its inner workings and judging it. For the true believer in any faith or ideology, recovery must pass through the abrasive abyss of radical skepticism and arrive at agnosticism. The inflated person is not an individuated human being. Retreat from this position of certitude and from the inner conviction of absolute righteousness is both humiliating and liberating. At such a juncture, the individuation imperative calls for taking stock, gaining psychological distance, reflecting, waking up from the nightmare and making a personal connection to the self as mandala. In the Chinese story, it means reconnecting to Tao like the rainmaker did when he stepped out of the city and withdrew into a hut for meditation and self-recollection. Minding the self requires detachment from partial self-figures in order to gain contact with the whole.

One can justly say that individuation speaks for a "new ethic" of psychological wholeness (Neumann 1949/1969), meaning too that it calls for reflection that does not submit to distracting and inflating archetypal patterns, images, values or ideas, but stands apart and retains the capacity to judge the very gods. Above them and beyond them, the self, as represented in the idea of Tao and the image of the mandala, supports the sense of an ethical stance contrary to the will to power and any sort of one-sided dominance by a single archetypal image or idea. The ethics of individuation transcends the moral codex of the community, also every form of simple adherence to the archetypal powers (the gods), and all other forms of identification with collective voices, politics, rules, images, or religious convictions. However, individuation is precisely not about going beyond good and evil *à la* Nietzsche's superman but rather about holding the opposites in tension and suffering the conflict. It calls for reflection and action under the protection and auspices of the self.

This movement into radical separation from strongly-held ideas and convictions leads to the second great movement of individuation, integration. The move here is toward inclusion of the complexity of the self within consciousness. It means acceptance of paradox and the polarities inherent in the psyche. This is recognition of (not identification with) a transcendent image of wholeness and unity, the self. To this, the ego personality submits as part of a greater whole and takes the role of servant on behalf of the self. This is how the Chinese rainmaker managed first to bring himself into harmony with Tao and through this to induce nature to follow. The ego serving the self also serves the world.

As shown, the individuation process has an inherent ethical dimension in both of its major movements, separation and integration. As the individual personality individuates, it inevitably becomes more deeply ethical and thereby contributes to the social and natural order, even if only indirectly and synchronistically. However, the collective ethical sense of societies and cultures also needs to individuate. By individuation of ethics, I refer to the further incarnation of the archetypal idea of justice, a transcendent moral order, within the human community. Since this development of the ethical requires the extension of ethical reflection into territories where it has not been considered before, especially with respect to individual situations and differences as well as to new cultural and scientific developments, experience tells us that this work is best done within communities and by people skilled in this kind of reflection.

The elaboration of ethics is a fully conscious undertaking, although its initial impetus and deepest grounding are unconscious and archetypal. Intuitions and dreams of justice precede codes and laws. These come to individuals through intuition or spontaneous emotional reactions. Hammering out the implications of such feelings and intuitions, however, is the work of conscious reflection among many people and over long periods of time. Traditions and cultures are made out of these communal reflections and the resulting teachings and moral codes. It is practically impossible for the involved individual to attain the necessary objectivity required for this type of complex reflection. The moral archetype of justice, raised to consciousness in community by individuals and elaborated by the reflection of many people upon unique and new situations, can thereby achieve further incarnation in new areas of experience and application. Collective reflection also prevents individual hubris and inflation from taking hold and distorting the outcome. This development of ethical awareness becomes a matter of urgent importance when individual and cultural/social developments critically outstrip collective consciousness and bring into question spheres of human activity and behavior where ethical considerations and viewpoints have not been elaborated yet.

This was the case, for example, with respect to psychoanalysis and psychotherapy in the early years of the twentieth century, when the kinds of relationship developed within these contexts were new and unfamiliar. It took several decades until ethics caught up and elaborated detailed codes of conduct for therapists that took into account the nuances and subtleties of transference and countertransference, areas of psychological sensitivity and vulnerability that had not been considered before. Dual and multiple relationships had to be noticed and reflected upon from the viewpoint of analytic understandings of transference. In recent decades, ethical codes and guidelines have emerged to cover these novel situations, to ensure fair treatment of patients in the sensitive positions they experience during psychotherapy (Solomon 2004).

On a broader social scale in our time, at least in Western cultures, the rise and advancement of feminism, consensual and long-term homosexual relationships, and medical advances (such as those having to do with extension and termination of life under dire circumstances, assisted pregnancy, genetic engineering, etc.) have called for profound reflections and debates on the ethical issues involved and implied. These reflections are on-going and far from complete. All revolve around questions of individuation and responsibility to self and others, the fundamental issue being justice (Frankena 1973: 46-52). Practically speaking, many cultural values play a role in how ethical awareness is expressed within a given context, but in the long run they are less decisive than the archetypal idea of justice and the eternal pressure to incarnate it more fully into cultural life. The on-going incarnation of the archetypal idea of justice is the individuation of ethics.

Chapter 14

The gifts of cultural dialogue

Contemporary spirituality is made of many parts. Mostly I have emphasized here personal experiences, such as dreams, visions and synchronistic experiences as material that goes into the warp and woof of this enterprise of minding the self. But there are also outside sources of inspiration, which contain important content and offer approaches that can lead the individuation process forward toward full incarnation of the self. In modern times, many people have learned from the world's religious traditions and combined what they find there with their own religious backgrounds and traditions to form a unique blend of approaches to the spiritual life. In the West, it has been the case for at least two centuries that Eastern religions have been included in the cultural matrix. This trend was certainly evident in Jung's thinking. West and East are coming together more and more on a common ground in modern spirituality.

Today, dialogues among cultures take place in many venues and on a multitude of levels. The net result of such dialogues is, however, very elusive and hard to define. Often such dialogue amounts to little more than a contest for dominance – who can shout the loudest and listen the least? The result often seems to be a standoff. At this stage in history, we are more or less in the middle of a learning process and still quite far from the end of it. The main problem has to do with careful listening to the other before responding with one's own views. The next challenge beyond hearing will be integrating the other's point of view into one's own perspective, i.e. letting the other viewpoint expand one's conceptions and enlarge one's cultural field of awareness. Minding the self in the large sense of the word requires listening to others who speak for what is unconscious to oneself but belongs to one's human wholeness. They represent the collective unconscious speaking.

What I am concerned with here above all is a dialogue about different perspectives on psychological and spiritual development, in short, about how intercultural dialogue may affect individuation. In this and the next chapter, I will address some aspects of Chinese philosophy and religion and attempt to link them to Jungian psychology and the individuation process. It is in the interest of humanity to foster greater consciousness among all people of the world, and to get there we need to pay attention to differences and to learning from each other. No single culture has the corner on truth about individuation, even if the ultimate goal of this process is identical for all cultures, namely the full incarnation of the human potential for personality, including spiritual development.

As a possible model for this process of enlargement of consciousness through cultural dialogue, I will consider Jung's engagement with Chinese thought. If any culture on earth presents the Eurocentric mind with radical otherness, it is the Chinese. The story of how Jung engaged Chinese thought is instructive. I believe he opened himself to its influence quite profoundly, while maintaining his Western roots in scientific thinking and clinical practice.

The Chinese influence on Jung received a strong impetus from his friendship in the 1920s with the German Protestant minister and Sinologist, Richard Wilhelm. Thomas Kirsch, upon the occasion of an historic first visit to China by an IAAP official in 1994, in a talk entitled "Jung and Tao", told the audience that Jung "claimed that Wilhelm had influenced him more than any other individual in his life. This comes as a surprise to many who would naturally have thought that Freud was the most influential person in Jung's development" (Kirsch 1998: 1).

Richard Wilhelm was born on May 10 1873 in Stuttgart, Germany. His father, a craftsman, died when Richard was nine years old, leaving the family in grave financial straits (Ballin 2002: 5). His mother and grandmother raised him along with his younger sister, Helene, until, in 1891, at the age of 18, he began theological studies at the University of Tübingen. Four years later he was ordained and became a vicar in a couple of small German villages, eventually being settled in Bad Boll under the supervision of the liberal Pastor Christoph Blumhardt in 1897. There he met his future wife, Salome Blumhardt, his mentor's daughter. They were engaged in 1899 just before Richard left for China to work in the Allgemein Protestantischer Missionsverein in the German colonial city of Qingdao (Tsingtao). A year later, Salome joined him in China, and they were married in Shanghai in 1900. Four children, all boys, followed in fairly rapid succession.

From 1899 until 1920, with a couple of brief periods back in Germany, Wilhelm worked in Qingdao as a pastor, educator, and translator. After arriving there, he quickly developed a fascination for Chinese culture and religion. In a short time he became fluent in the Chinese language and began translating Chinese texts into German. His first publications, among them works by Confucius, Da Hüo, Tsai-Li-Sekte, and a Chinese astronomy text, date from 1905 onward. After World War I, in 1920, Wilhelm returned with his family to Germany, but in two years he was back in China, this time in Peking, where he served as scientific counselor in the German embassy and taught at Peking University. Returning permanently to Germany in 1924, he became professor of Chinese history and philosophy at the University of Frankfurt and remained in this position until his death in 1930, just shy of his fifty-seventh birthday.

A prolific writer, his most important published works were translations from the Chinese and commentaries on Chinese texts. Between 1910 and 1930, he worked on translating and editing an eight-volume series of classic Chinese texts entitled *Religion und Philosophie Chinas* ('The Religion and Philosophy of China'). His translations into German, published by the prestigious house Eugen Diederichs in Jena, brought him considerable recognition in his home country and established his reputation as a leading German Sinologist. For ten years, he worked in close collaboration with the noted Chinese scholar and sage, Lao Nai-hsuan (1843-1921), to produce his much-admired translation of the *I Ching* in 1924. After his final return to Germany in 1924, he became known as "the spiritual link between China and Europe" (Rennstich 1998: 1301). He enjoyed friendly contact with numerous culturally prominent figures of the time – among them Rudolph Otto, Count Hermann Keyserling, Albert Schweitzer, Herman Hesse, Martin Buber, Tagore, and, most importantly for our purposes, C.G. Jung. With Jung the relationship turned into a close friendship. They were, they found, kindred spirits.

The correspondence on file in the ETH's C.G. Jung Archive is a brief one, covering a period of only about ten months and containing 13 letters. It represents a brief fragment of their relationship, which extended over nearly a decade all told. Some letters between the two men are obviously missing from this scant collection. The first one is a letter from Wilhelm to Jung dated December 28 1928. The letterhead reads "China-Institut, Frankfort a. M, Director: Prof. Dr. Richard Wilhelm". In a formal and typically correct style, Wilhelm asks Jung if he would be willing to let his name be used as a sponsor of the newly founded *International Institut für Buddhismusforschung* (International Institute for the Study of Buddhism). This Institute was founded by a committee at the *Musée Guimet* in Paris under the inspiration of S.E. Tai Hsü, President of the Chinese Buddhist Union, which also had centers in Nanking and Singapore.

It is unclear from the available correspondence what sort of relationship Jung and Wilhelm had prior to this letter. From their previous encounters and discussions, Wilhelm would have recognized that Jung had a deep interest in Eastern, and particularly in Chinese, thought and religion, including Buddhism. Jung writes that he met Wilhelm "in the early 1920s" (Jung 1950/1969: par. 966), and most likely this introduction took place at Graf Keyserling's "School of Wisdom" in Darmstadt, where Wilhelm was invited to give lectures and Jung was sometimes in attendance. (Keyserling had visited Wilhelm in China and was impressed with his broad interest in world religions, Keyserling's specialty.) In 1921 Wilhelm also gave a talk on the *I Ching* at the Psychological Club in Zurich, Jung's home ground. Without doubt, Jung would have been among the first purchasers of Wilhelm's translation of the *I Ching* in 1924. In his "Forward" to the English translation of the *I Ching*, Jung states that he had been familiar with Legge's translation before he found Wilhelm's, so his interest in this book preceded his meeting Wilhelm and perhaps whetted his interest in Chinese thought in preparation for what he would later discover with Wilhelm. In May 1926, Wilhelm again lectured at the Psychological Club in Zurich. His lectures this time were titled *Chinesische Joga-praxis* ('Chinese Yoga Practice') and *Chinesische Seelenlehre* ('Chinese Spiritual Teachings'). Jung, just back from his long African expedition, was in all likelihood present for these lectures. In summary, it is clear that by the time the first letter in the extant correspondence arrived on Jung's doorstep in 1928, the two men had had a considerable exchange of views and would have built up a relationship based on mutual interest in Chinese philosophy and Eastern religions.

The second letter in the ETH collection is from Jung to Wilhelm, dated April 6 1929. Jung addresses Wilhelm as *Mein lieber Professor* (My Dear Professor), a somewhat more familiar form than the formal German greeting, *Sehr geehrter Professor* (Highly Esteemed Professor), which indicates a somewhat personal relationship. His letter is friendly and quite casual in style. He says that he hopes Wilhelm is feeling better after his visit to Zurich: "It was surely the cold mayonnaise at X's which ruined our care" (Jung 1973: 63). On January 29, Wilhelm had given a lecture at the Psychological Club, now his third appearance there, entitled *Einige Probleme der Buddhistischen Meditation* ('Some Problems with Buddhist Meditation'). Jung goes on in his letter to say that he will be passing through Frankfurt on his way to Bad Nauheim for a Psychotherapy Congress (the 4th General Medical Congress for Psychotherapy, where he would deliver his lecture, 'The Aims of Psychotherapy' – cf. Jung 1931/1966), and would like to meet with Wilhelm if possible, however briefly. He would have a three-hour stopover in Frankfurt between trains. He also mentions a joint project: "I shall soon be able to make a start on our MS" (Jung 1973: 63). This is a reference to *The Secret of the Golden Flower*, a text that would eventually be published with a psychological commentary by Jung. It seems that Wilhelm sent his German translation of *Golden Flower* to Jung sometime in 1928. So, by this point, we find Jung and Wilhelm deep into an intellectual partnership – "*our* MS". Jung also suggests to Wilhelm that he take a retreat to get away from too much work, and he asks: "Why are there no secular monasteries for people who ought to be living outside time? The world eats them up from inside if it doesn't from outside" (Jung 1973: 63). Jung must have been aware of Wilhelm's fragile physical condition. He would die one year later.

In fact, *The Secret of the Golden Flower*, an obscure and little-known text of Chinese alchemy, stimulated a critical turning point for Jung. In *Memories, Dreams, Reflections*, he writes: "Light on the nature of alchemy began to come to me only after I had read the text of the *Golden Flower*, that specimen of Chinese alchemy which Richard Wilhelm sent me..." (Jung 1963a: 204). Jung's fascination with alchemy began, according to Jung himself, with this Chinese treatise, and he would spend the next 30 years deeply immersed in the study of alchemy.

What he found in the Chinese treatise was a set of images and inner developments that ran parallel to what he had found in the analysis of some of his Western patients and, most importantly, in his own experiences of the individuation process as recorded in *The Red Book*. In the Chinese alchemy text, he glimpsed the basic patterns of psychological and spiritual development that constitute the archetypal process of individuation. From Chinese alchemy he would go on and enter into a deep study of alchemical symbolism, primarily in Western sources, interpreting and translating them into psychological categories and raising the formulas and imagery to a level of consciousness that is suited to the modern mind, while at the same time relating these symbols and images to the deep unconscious structures, processes, and symbolic representations offered by the psyches of modern people in analysis.

Through his relationship with Wilhelm, Jung allowed the influences of Chinese thought to enter into his own theorizing about the archetypal basis of the human psyche. The dialogue between East and West in Jung's mind contributed to a new concept of psychic process and wholeness that applies to all of humanity. Through this type of deeply-reflected dialogue, the universals of the human mind can be uncovered and the way prepared for the possibility of a new global culture in which all of humanity can participate.

The third letter in the correspondence (Jung to Wilhelm dated April 26 1929) opens with an apology for intruding on Wilhelm's privacy by rushing to his home while passing through Frankfurt on his way to Bad Nauheim. He says that he was worried about Wilhelm's health. Again we see that Jung must have sensed Wilhelm's physical frailty. Jung expresses his urgent concern by underlining two words in his message: "You are *too important* to our Western world. I must keep telling you this. You mustn't melt away or otherwise disappear, or get ill" (Jung 1973: 63). Then he comes to the point of his letter:

> The result of my lecture at the Nauheim Psychotherapeutic Congress is that, without my previous knowledge, the board of the Psychotherapeutic Society has decided to ask *you* to give a lecture next year (presumably in Baden-Baden). This will make history! Think what it means if medical practitioners, who get at the ordinary person so brashly and in the most vulnerable spot, were to be inoculated with Chinese philosophy! It is simply inconceivable. I am delighted and only hope that no devils will keep you away from this historic occasion. This really goes to the heart of the matter. Medicine is switching over to psychology with a vengeance,

and that's where the East comes in. There's nothing to be done with the theologians and philosophers because of their arrogance.

(Jung 1973: 64-65)

Here we can see the gravity that Jung attached to Wilhelm's transmission of Chinese philosophy to the West. The transformation of medicine that Jung speaks of here was his lifelong concern, namely, to shift psychiatry and the mental health professions specifically, away from the dominant materialistic orientation of the medical model to a psychological and spiritual orientation. For this, he had looked to many academic disciplines in the previous decades, and now he glimpsed a rich and powerful resource in Chinese thought. This perception that Chinese philosophy and religion could be a potent tool for bringing about the transformation of Western medicine, especially in its attitude toward the treatment of mental illness, was founded on Jung's conviction that in its deep historic introspective tradition Chinese alchemy had discovered universal aspects of the psyche, and this discovery could be added to Western findings to contribute to a more effective approach for eliciting the full potential for human individuation.

At the end of this letter, Jung states in passing: "The Lamaic mandala has been copied. I will send back the original soon" (Jung 1973: 64). In *Memories, Dreams, Reflections*, he comments at some length on what this image meant for him. He relates that as a part of his own self analysis and inner work, he painted a couple of images that he would later call mandalas, and one of these he says had an odd Chinese quality to it (Jung 1963a: 197). Shortly after finishing this picture, he writes:

> I received a letter from Richard Wilhelm enclosing the manuscript of a Taoist alchemical treatise entitled *The Secret of the Golden Flower*, with a request that I write a commentary on it. I devoured the text at once, for the text gave me undreamed of confirmation of my ideas about the mandala and the circumambulation of the center. That was the first event which broke through my isolation... In remembrance of this coincidence, this 'synchronicity', I wrote underneath the picture which had made so Chinese an impression upon me: 'In 1928, when I was painting this picture, show- ing the golden, well-fortified castle, Richard Wilhelm in Frankfort sent me the thousand-year-old Chinese text on the yellow castle, the germ of the immortal body'.

(Jung 1963a: 197)

What *The Secret of the Golden Flower* suggested was that psychological devel- opment is not linear but rather spiral, a circumambulation of a non-representable center: "There is no linear evolution; there is only circumambulation of the self.

Uniform development exists, at most, only at the beginning; later, everything points toward the center" (Jung 1963a: 196-97). This notion of individuation as circular or spiral rather than linear, basically a Chinese view, would become a central feature of Jung's theory of individuation. Chinese thought, therefore, played a key role in coming to this understanding and formulation of a process that is perhaps the centerpiece of Jung's psychological theory. It was precisely the absence of strictly linear thinking in Chinese philosophy that impressed Jung.

At the time of the correspondence, of course, Jung had no idea of how important the long-range influence and effect of Wilhelm's friendship and gifts would be for him. His intuition led him, however, to use the word "historic" when speaking of Wilhelm's potential contribution to medical psychotherapy. This is because he sensed the transformative potential of what Chinese thought had to offer to the materialism and rationalism of Western medical science. Chinese thought, as delivered to European culture by Richard Wilhelm, would further an historic transformation. With respect to Jung's own thinking, at least, this seems to have been the case.

The next letter in the correspondence, dated May 25 1929, is short but quite moving and indicates a new level in the personal relationship between the two men. Again, there seems to be a letter missing from Wilhelm to Jung in the extant correspondence, since Jung writes back to Wilhelm celebrating his acceptance of the invitation to give the lecture proposed by Jung a month earlier. For the first time in the correspondence, he addresses Wilhelm as "Dear Friend". He writes: "Dear Friend, It is lovely to hear the word 'friend' from you. Fate seems to have apportioned to us the role of two piers which support the weight of the bridge between East and West. I thank you with all my heart that you have agreed to give the lecture" (Jung 1973: 66). The lost letter from Wilhelm must have invited this new level of closeness between them, and Jung responded with feeling and the image of a joint mission assigned by fate to bridge East and West. The remarkable thing is that Jung locates himself in this way. It was obvious that Wilhelm was such a mediating figure for Europeans. But Jung? Jung's role would be somewhat different from Wilhelm's, as it turned out. Always he begins his reflections and interpretations of non-Western materials from the point of view of the Westerner, with his own experience as a primary reference point. Wilhelm stands more completely in the Chinese mentality. Whereas Wilhelm, the learned Sinologist, had spent nearly 25 years living and working in China, Jung was a Western psychiatrist who spent his entire life in Switzerland. But the meeting with Wilhelm struck a deep chord, and he was importantly changed by the relationship.

Jung's method for mediating East and West called for him to stick with the Western psyche and to find points of commonality with Eastern thought as revealed in its classical texts. Wilhelm was a Christian missionary who had so deeply immersed himself in Chinese thought that he engaged the West from a classical and ancient Chinese point of view. Knowing the philosophy and religion of both sides, he could critique his own religious tradition from a Chinese perspective. His translations of Chinese texts into German are more than technical translations. They present the content in such a way that it can be effectively received by the Western mind. A point of criticism has been that his translation of the *I Ching* is not literal and exact enough, but his transformation of the text also makes it more accessible. Wilhelm was hermetic, a brilliant communicator as well as a translator.

In the same letter, Jung again expresses his concern about Wilhelm's health. Given that Wilhelm had agreed to give the lecture the following year to the Medical Psychotherapy Society, Jung wanted to be sure that he would follow through. (In fact, he would not be around to give that lecture. He died a couple of months before it was due to be presented.) Jung also apologizes in his letter for not yet completing his commentary on *The Secret of the Golden Flower*, and writes: "No harm has been done by my putting it off, because I have had a number of experiences that have given me some very valuable insights" (Jung 1973: 66). Actually, Jung had become personally engaged in studying the text far beyond his original intent.

In the months following this exchange, Wilhelm received some treatments for his health problems, and the correspondence turns to the minutiae of publishing – contracts, fees, etc. and some further projects being planned. Then on September 10 1929 Jung writes to Wilhelm from Bollingen and announces that the commentary "is more or less finished" (Jung 1973: 67). It is longer than expected "because it represents a European reaction to the wisdom of China. I have tried my hand at interpreting Tao" (Jung 1973: 67). In the commentary as it is finally published, Jung offers a rich and nuanced psychological interpretation of the Chinese alchemical text and relates his own and his patients' inner development to the processes described in it. In both the Chinese text and the inner experience of Western patients, he writes, the goal of the work is greater consciousness and wholeness. We see that, on both sides, minding the self is the chief concern and project. Jung puts the emphasis in his commentary decidedly upon living the Tao rather than only speaking about it or studying books about it. Jung's essay is a *tour de force* and must be ranked as one of his most brilliant and inspired works. The careful methodology he lays out and employs here is one that he will carry forward in his work over the decades to follow. While Wilhelm bridges from China to Europe with his translation, Jung bridges from Europe to China with his psychological commentary. Between them, they did truly create a splendid avenue for exchange and discourse between East and West. It is a model of deep and effective dialogue with astonishing results.

In the penultimate letter of the correspondence, dated October 24 1929, Wilhelm suggests some minor changes in Jung's text and in the contract with the publisher. He also confirms that the German title of the book will be *Das Geheimnis der Goldenen Blüte* (*The Secret of the Golden Flower*). A Chinese editor had wanted to change it to "The Art of Prolonging Human Life" to make it more popular and marketable, but they wisely decided to go back to the original title and retain the mystery.

In the final letter, dated October 28 1929, Jung states his agreement with the changes and expresses his strong approval of the title as suggested by Wilhelm. He also says that he is preparing a series of mandalas drawn by patients: "The pictures complement one another and by their very variety give an excellent picture of the efforts of the European unconscious to grasp the eschatology of the East" (Jung 1973: 71). "Eschatology" is the goal: the creation of wholeness and conscious incarnation of the self, or building "the diamond body" in the language of Chinese alchemy. This is the net result of a careful minding of the self. Jung closes the correspondence with the prescient sentence: "In any event you should never forget to spare your body, as the spirit has the unpleasant quality of wanting to eat the body up" (Jung 1973: 71). The book was published at the end of 1929. Wilhelm passed away on March 1 1930.

In May 1930, Jung delivered the principal address at a memorial service for Richard Wilhelm in Munich, Germany. In tribute to his friend, Jung expresses his deep gratitude for what he received from Wilhelm: "Wilhelm's life-work is of such immense importance to me because it clarified and confirmed so much that I had been seeking, striving for, thinking, and doing in my efforts to alleviate the psychic sufferings of Europeans. It was a tremendous experience for me to hear through him, in clear language, things I had dimly divined in the confusion of our European unconscious. Indeed, I feel myself so very much enriched by him that it seems to me as if I had received more from him than from any other man" (Jung 1930/1966: para. 96). Jung then tells the assembly of friends why he feels Wilhelm's contribution was so important: his translation of and commentary on the *I Ching* provides "an Archimedean point from which our Western attitude of mind could be lifted off its foundations" (Jung 1930/1966: para. 78). Moreover, he "has inoculated us with the living germ of the Chinese spirit, capable of working a fundamental change in our view of the world" (Jung 1930/1966: para. 78). The *I Ching* is based not on the principle of causality but on the principle of synchronicity, a term Jung uses for the first time in this Memorial Address, and this is precisely what Jung thought Western science needed to complete its worldview. He would propose this idea formally some 20 years later in a volume published with the renowned physicist, Wolfgang Pauli (Jung and Pauli 1952/1955).

The treasures that Jung found in Chinese thought, thanks to the inspiration of Richard Wilhelm and his translations, continued to influence his thinking for the rest of his life. What began in their joint mission of holding up a bridge between East and West ended in a complex psychological theory that combines Western linear, causal, scientific thinking and Eastern (i.e. Chinese) non-causal, synchronistic, holistic thinking. In such works as *Aion*, 'Synchronicity: An Acausal Connecting Principle', and *Mysterium Coniunctionis*, Jung proposes a view of psychic reality that bridges between European scientific thinking and Chinese Taoist thinking.

In his life, too, Jung used himself to unite these "opposites", East and West. He did attempt to live the Tao and not only to think and write about it. The influence of China entered into his everyday life as well as into his psychological theorizing. I believe this has continued, to some extent at least, in the clinical tradition that is a central part of analytical psychology.

Chapter 15

Minding the self

Individuation and the emergence of spirituality can take place in almost every phase of life, in dimensions of course dependent on the stage of psychological and cognitive development at the time. An especially fertile ground for new developments in both psychological and spiritual dimensions, however, forms during periods of crisis, in other words "in difficult times". The emotional upheaval and confusion that characterize such short or long periods in life find people thrown into states of anxiety, depression and inner turmoil when suddenly they realize how adrift they really are, how ungrounded and lost. This realization may be the beginning of wisdom if it becomes a window into existential truth, and therefore an occasion for deeper than usual self-examination. One may come to question the meaning of personal life as it had been felt or conceived before and to doubt the validity of self-told narratives invented in the past. As self-satisfying images break down, people find themselves stranded in a fog of confusion and uncertainty. One speaks softly then of a "loss of soul". Paradoxically, however, it is in such difficult times of crisis that new psychological developments become more possible. In happy and easy times, one is less likely to look for deeper truths. Crisis changes this and can be the motivating force for pursuing greater self-awareness and consciousness.

C.G. Jung recorded his experiences of individuation in such difficult times in *The Red Book*. We can learn much directly from Jung's account, but it may be helpful to place his experience in the perspective of other spiritual traditions and thus broaden the horizon. These parallels can help us not only to understand Jung a little better but also to orient our minds in purposive directions that do not rest upon a specific biography. To this end, I will consult a well-known classic text of Zen Buddhism that offers a brilliant summary of the individuation process, "The Ten Ox-Herding Pictures" originally drawn by the Chinese Chan (Zen) master Kuo-an Shih-yuan in the twelfth century. Here, however, I will use images of the paintings of this series by Shuhbun (1454), which are now kept in the Shokukuji-Temple in Kyoto.[1] This famous Buddhist teaching text is familiar to many people in the West because of D.T. Suzuki's books on Zen Buddhism, which brought the Ox-Herding

Pictures to the attention of a large public in mid-twentieth century. These pictures lend us a suggestive instrument for understanding key individuation experiences and placing them in a developmental pattern. Here, I am of course lifting these pictures out of the Zen Buddhist meditation context and placing them into a depth psychological one. What matters, though, is that the Zen pictures can teach us something useful about individuating in difficult times and about minding the self.

The concept of individuation in Jungian psychology, it should be remembered, embraces the development of consciousness in all of its stages, in conjunction with the emergence of the self in its full complexity. Paying attention to this process is what I am referring to with the phrase "minding the self". This denotes lifting the deeply-embedded psychological patterns of individuation to the level of the conscious mind and therefore making them available for reflection and extraction of meaning. This process takes place over the course of an entire lifetime. In fact, it is never completed even though it continues even into deep old age and up to the very end of a lifetime, possibly extending even beyond our biological existence.

The Ten Ox-Herding Pictures illustrate important features of individuation, albeit in a much abbreviated form, and the series can be seen to go hand in hand with images and passages from Jung's *Red Book*, which I will mention as the Zen story unfolds. Many commentaries have been written about the Ox-Herding Pictures and the brief texts that go with them. I will not recapitulate what others have said but rather reflect on the pictures as significant moments in the individuation process as we know it from contemporary experience in and out of Jungian psychoanalysis and read about it in *The Red Book*. The ten pictures in the series offer an excellent means for thinking about the individuation process during difficult times, while Jung's *Red Book* shows an abundance of details and a methodology.

The series begins by showing us a man obviously distraught. I imagine him at his wit's end. He has lost his ox and is desperately looking for it. The first picture is titled "Seeking the Ox" (Figure 15.1).

The brief poetic text accompanying it reads:

> Wandering through bushes in search of something,
>   so huge a lake and high a mountain
> Looms before my eyes in the far distance -
>   my journey seems never to end.
> Completely worn out, nothing
>   have I found, not a single clue.
> All I hear is the chirp of a cicada
>   hanging on a maple tree;
> It tells me summer is ending.
>   (tr. Yuri Yoshikawa)

Figure 15.1 Seeking the ox.

This is the condition of someone struggling, weary but determined. He stumbles about in the confusion of "wandering through bushes in search of something", and so reminds us of other pilgrims, like Dante at midlife who got lost in a wood and so began his journey through the Inferno to beatific visions in Paradiso. This man has fallen into difficult times and is looking for something of value, now lost.

From a psychological perspective, we would suppose that he has lost contact with the self. It is a "loss of soul" and therefore engenders anxiety and depressed affect. Typically this happens when a person loses a loved one who has carried an essential part of the soul for them in projection. Someone who loses contact with the self suffers lack of energy for normal life. Basic animal instinct has gone missing. This amounts to being cut off from the source of energy and spirit in the unconscious, and a person feels under-standably anxious when separated from deeper levels of the self. Consciousness finds itself isolated and without grounding in instinct, even the instinct for life itself. So we understand that the ox represents a connec-tion to the man's unconscious instinctual life force, the source of his libido.

He has lost contact with his "primal nature", as Roshi Kapleau comments: "It is probably because of the sacred nature of the ox in ancient India that this animal came to be used to symbolize man's primal nature or Buddha-mind" (Kapleau 1980: 313). For the Buddhist, primal nature and Buddha-mind are synonymous. With depth psychology it is somewhat other, since the self includes the physical and instinctual aspects of the psyche as shown clearly in *Systema munditotius* (see Chapter 11). It falls upon the ox-herder now to find and restore his connection to the self. The individuation journey begins with a regression of libido: the man goes into the forest in search of his ox, that is, into his own nature and inner world. He decides to explore the unconscious.

The text does not tell us why this has happened to this particular man. Since this is an archetypal story, it speaks of Everyone, and we do know that this is what often occurs in troubled times when people are struck by sudden loss and trauma. This can fall suddenly upon entire families, clans and nations when they are devastated by traumatic events on a large scale, such as terrorism, war or natural calamity. Suddenly they find themselves bereft, without purpose or interest in living on, engulfed by despair and anxiety, without a guiding myth if religious conviction also abandons them. People become frighteningly disoriented and desperate. They are at a loss. Where should they turn? We know that to move forward out of this crisis, one needs to find a sense of hope and purpose and a symbol to bring energy back to go on living a creative and meaningful life, but how is one to do this? This is a decidedly dangerous moment because people are tempted to grasp at straws, to find anything or anyone to blame, or to tie themselves to someone who promises to lead them out of the sorry state of disarray and crippling anxiety. Tricksters and phony political leaders will offer images of hope and promises of deliverance. Often, too, this is the emotional condition of people who come seeking for help from psychotherapists. Perhaps people living with spiritual traditions like Zen Buddhism will undertake a period of strenuous meditation – a "time out" – to go deeper and to rediscover their connection to the primal self. One way or another, some people will find that they must go in search of the lost ox and not just give up on life, fall into addictions, run after hucksters, or commit suicide. Some people will go within and begin the quest, and these are the ones who have a chance to use a personal crisis for further individuation.

This first picture perfectly illustrates Jung's condition when he began to write the entries into his journal that would later become *The Red Book*. At the outset he cries: "My soul, where are you? I speak; I call you – are you there?" (Jung 2009: 232). His journey inward begins with an anguished call for what has been lost, the soul, his link to the self. He is a man looking desperately for his lost equivalent of the ox. In his suffering and confusion, he begins a journey into the unknown.

As he confesses in *Memories, Dreams, Reflections*, Jung realized that he had lost his own way by going down the Freudian path and, now separated from Freud and his followers, he came to the stark realization that he had no myth whatsoever to live by (Jung 1963a: 171). This grim realization motivated him to go in search of his soul. In the painting that opens 'Liber Primus' in *The Red Book*, we see a typical Swiss landscape with village and mountains in the background, and in the foreground a ship is preparing to set out on a voyage. This depicts the beginning of a long journey, and it is the equivalent of the first picture in the Ox-Herding series. Anxiously setting out to discover the whereabouts of something essential that is lost, Jung embarks on a search for it. In *The Red Book* we can observe how he conducted this exploration. Mainly, he used the method of active imagination, which is a practice similar to meditation. Active imagination moves from image to image as they emerge spontaneously into consciousness. It is a method that many people after Jung have also found useful for undertaking the search for their own soul in difficult times.

In the second picture of the Ox-Herding series, titled "Finding the Tracks", we see the man carefully following traces of the vanished ox (Figure 15.2).

Figure 15.2 Finding the tracks.

He has caught sight of a hint of where the symbol may be found and is following the tracks. Now there is a glimmer of hope for re-establishing contact with the primal self. This is the earliest sign of the approach of what the alchemists called "albedo", the stage of the opus following upon "nigredo", an indeterminably long dark night of the soul.

In the practice of active imagination, this corresponds to the startling moment when imagination comes to life, and imaginal figures begin to show autonomy. Something unexpected and unplanned begins to happen. There is movement. Jung recorded such a critically-important moment in *The Red Book*. He describes how he entered a cave and found a stone with an opening in it that looked down to an underground river in which he saw some figures floating, among them the head of a man and a black scarab beetle; a red sun radiated the water from beneath (Jung 2009: 237). Small paintings in "Liber Primus" depict this scene. This was a critical moment because it was the first time he came into such vivid contact with autonomous images of the unconscious, which would lead to more figures as he proceeded. Before this, his lost soul had come into view and there were some dialogues with her, but the quality of the images was somewhat vague, and to the reader this seems like an interior dialogue more or less confined to the domain of consciousness, not reaching very far into the unconscious – a beginning, but pale by comparison with what is to come. In the chapter titled, "Descent into the Hell of the Future", we come upon a dramatic shift in tone. Here imagination powerfully takes the lead, and the protagonist begins to enter the territory of the psyche to a depth not discovered before. The psychological situation begins to change in this moment of the process, and now a convincing project gets underway. The reality of the psyche begins to be felt consciously, and there is no turning back.

The third picture in the series, titled "Catching Sight of the Ox", shows the man in hot pursuit of his ox, now found (Figure 15.3).

He is coming closer and the excitement is palpable. In *The Red Book*, this state of affairs is depicted when several figures appear to the Protagonist, such as the couple Elijah and Salome. These living images bring insight and new life, and they will play a significant role in his further individuation process. This is a moment that proves decisively that the individuation process is working. It is more than the hint observed in the previous picture. In *The Red Book* narrative, living figures now emerge spontaneously out of the dark background of the psyche. In psychotherapy, this is when sessions come alive and the space between therapist and client becomes charged with psychic energy. The individuation process is now working and fully underway. The energy becomes palpable. Symbols become alive and available. They are convincing and have considerably more weight than mere metaphors and figures of speech. It is the difference between a living ox and a set of distant images barely glimpsed. A psychic realm opens that Jung names an "intermediate realm", a "place or the

Figure 15.3 Catching sight of the ox.

medium of realization [that] is neither mind nor matter, but that intermediate realm of subtle reality that can be adequately only expressed by the symbol. The symbol is neither abstract nor concrete, neither rational nor irrational, neither real nor unreal. It is always both: it is *non vulgi*, the aristocratic preoccupation of one who is set apart (*cuiuslibet sequestrate*), chosen and predestined by God from the very beginning" (Jung 1944/1968: para. 400). It is this intermediate realm, where contents are expressed strictly in the form of symbols, that the imaginative activity of individuation hereafter takes place. It is a realm where the questions, "Is it real?" "Is it true or false?" etc., have no place. It has its own standing and its own ground. This picture signals entry into the intermediate realm of the symbolic. This is decisive for further movement in the individuation process.

In the fourth picture, we see the man actually catching up with the ox and capturing it (Figure 15.4).

Here he is shown in contact with the primal self. Without the opening of the intermediate realm, this would not be possible. Now a genuine relationship can be negotiated, albeit with strenuous effort, because the game is real.

Figure 15.4 Capturing the ox.

A possibility has developed now that the primal self can be held fast, more or less, and therefore eventually incarnated into conscious everyday life, which we will see taking place in the following pictures. This picture is taut with energy. It shows an *agon*, a colossal struggle, to bring the two sides together and into a stable relationship. The ego is now in a position to establish a strong and enduring contact with primal self, albeit one still of struggle and conflict at this point. While there remains great tension in the relationship, it is now possible to conceive of a stable connection in the future. The rope that holds them together is the transcendent function, a term that has been explicated in previous chapters. Ego and self are not in harmony, but they are in contact. The struggle is engaged between the ego and larger, stronger, contrary tendencies active in the psyche.

The Red Book is replete with passages where we find Jung locked into such fierce struggle with figures of the unconscious. Frequently, Soul shows her independence and does not adjust herself to the wishes of the ego. There is debate and tension, the need for patience, for more suffering. The ego must learn from the soul, and they must negotiate a relationship that will be acceptable

Figure 15.5 Taming the ox.

to both. It is not easy. It does not yield to a quick fix. In practice, this struggle with oneself – with the shadow, with instincts that pull in different directions from ego preferences, with anima and animus attitudes that contradict the ego – can last for a long time before a person arrives at the more integrated position of picture five.

The fifth picture, titled "Taming the Ox", reflects a further stage in the building up of the transcendent function until it is in functioning order (Figure 15.5).

A smooth and harmonious relationship can now develop gradually between the ego and the self. Here one sees that the rope is relaxed, and the contest of wills has subsided, so that, as shown in the sixth picture, the ox can even be ridden comfortably back to the place of the beginning. This picture, named "Riding the Ox Home", shows us a moment of tranquility in the individuation process (Figure 15.6).

Calm and harmony prevail. The relationship between man and ox is ideal, and both are content. The man, earlier so distraught and disoriented, now happily plays his flute. He has arrived at his goal. Or so it seems.

Figure 15.6 Riding the ox home.

The series might well stop here since what the man set out to do at the beginning has been accomplished. However, this is not enough. It is a respite, but it does not last forever and it is not stable, and so the process must continue. One can conjecture that it is at this point that traditional symbols become fixed and organized religions develop around them. Rituals, dogmas and icons never change. They are permanently set in place and are meant to maintain a stable relationship between the human and the divine. The spiritual life of the individual is different, however, marked with many ups and downs, advances and regressions, as the dynamic process moves on to levels that are rarely attained but may be glimpsed. We learn from *The Red Book* that the process of individuation is very long indeed and that it contains a great many ordeals. The Ox-Herding Pictures condense this long process of individuation into only ten images and wisely suggest that the process should not be fixed at the stage of harmony as shown in picture six. Many people get off here, however, and are satisfied to remain contained within collective religious structures and doctrines. It is a flight to stability and offers a comfort level that

Figure 15.7 Ox forgotten, self alone.

is appealing. The way ahead is extremely steep. Picture six shows us harmony and self-acceptance. The remaining four pictures press on to complete the journey.

After finding, capturing and taming the ox in the first six pictures, the remaining four pictures take the process to a supreme psychological and spiritual level of development that includes the transformation of the primal unconscious and its integration into a new type of consciousness. This is a kind of sublime spirituality that suggests the summit of full individuation, an unrealizable goal for everyday life but one that can be glimpsed and recorded in imagination and perhaps incarnated in life to an extent, if not completely. In pictures seven, eight and nine, we see the progressive initiation and entry into a state of consciousness that is utterly grounded in the self, embodied and without remainder. This is then extended in picture ten, which elevates the personality as a whole to the role of free participant in the world.

In picture seven (Figure 15.7), the ox has disappeared, leaving only the man in a posture of prayer. The title of this picture, according to Roshi Kapleau, is:

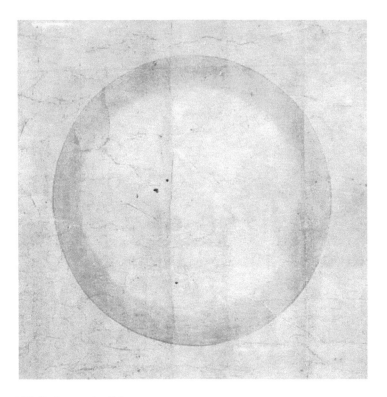

Figure 15.8 Both ox and self forgotten.

"Ox forgotten, self alone". Psychologically said, this might be: "Ox absorbed, sense of self made whole". The primal self has been absorbed into centered, meditative consciousness. Consciousness is now fully capable and adequate, and the wellspring of energy is available for devotion.

In the next picture, the man has vanished as well, leaving a scene of pure emptiness (Figure 15.8). Roshi Kapleau titles this: "Both ox and self forgotten."

In the ninth picture, we find a scene with objects but no ox and no man in it, with the highly suggestive title: "Return to the Source" (Figure 15.9). At the center of this trinity of symbolic pictures, which move from sublimation of the primal self to emptiness to unencumbered oneness with the cosmos – a brilliant summation of the fully-minded self – is an image for the numinous experience of sheer transcendent wholeness, depicted by the classic Zen Buddhist Ensō image. The poetic text for picture eight reads:

> Everything has disappeared – the whip in my hands,
>   the reins for the cattle, even I myself, and so my ox.

Figure 15.9 Return to the source.

> The blue sky spreads out so far and wide,
>   no answer can be found.
> How can snow survive in a blazing kiln?
> Finally, I comprehend the teaching
>   Of the ancient patriarch.
>   (tr. Yuri Yoshikawa)

This is a moment of awareness when "no answer can be found", but which includes comprehension of "the teaching of the ancient patriarch". This is not a vacuum but actually the opposite. As the text states: "Everything has disappeared." It indicates in fact a vision of fullness within the emptiness, of subtle and hidden unity among the elements that played a role in the previous pictures. It is an experience of the infinite without boundaries of any sort. It thus joins the individuating person's personality with the spirit of the patriarchs, the archetypes that inhabit the foundation of being. It is also a moment of transcendence over the artificial divisions between self and other and between body and mind. The previous picture, showing sublimation of the primal self, is the preparation for this state of oneness, and the following picture is the return of it into conscious life, but transformed. In fact, ego has been resolved into the self, and the person experiences reality without the interference of complexes and defenses. All evidence of ego anxiety has vanished, and so the fundamental psychological problem presented in the first picture is now completely and permanently resolved.

Glimpses of states of mind like this are an essential part of the individuation process. They carry us beyond the restrictive limitations of the ego and immerse consciousness in "the source". However, while they transform consciousness and make up an essential feature of the individuation process, they do not represent the final goal. This is recognized in The Ox-Herding Pictures. Picture eight, the Ensō image, does not represent the conclusion of the series. In picture nine, "Return to the Source", the individual goes even further and rests in a state of solid oneness with the self, which is in turn at one with the world. Jung speaks of this stage of the individuation process, using the alchemical language of Gerhard Dorn, as the third stage of the *mysterium coniunctionis* (Jung 1955/1963: paras. 759ff.). He writes: "This would consist, psychologically, in a synthesis of the conscious with the unconscious" (Jung 1955/1963: para. 770). Here the person is not only at one with the self as individually denominated but at one with the soul of the world, with "the potential world of the first day of creation" (Jung 1955/1963: para. 766), or, as the text for the ninth of the Ox-Herding Pictures states, with "the Source". It is a moment of oneness with the cosmos, without projection and without desire.

The tenth and final picture in the series is titled "Entering the Market Place", and it shows us that the young student-like figure of the first picture has been transformed into a sage (Figure 15.10).

In this depiction, he is shown in both forms, as youth and sage. We might think of this as reconciliation between *senex* and *puer aeternus*, or perhaps the sage is confronting his former self. At any rate, the text reads:

> He comes into the market bare-chested and barefooted;
> Though covered with dirt and dust, his face beams with delight.
> He doesn't use magic like a legendary wizard,
> But he makes dead trees bloom.
>
> (tr. Yuri Yoshikama)

The sage comes in with the magic of synchronicity and "he makes dead trees bloom". As with the Rainmaker story, nature responds to the sage's fructifying presence. He represents a type of consciousness that serves the world and belongs no longer to himself alone, but to humanity and to the world.

The individuation process, as we know it in practice, runs through many cycles. Jung speaks of a continuous "circumambulation of the self" (Jung

Figure 15.10 Entering the market place.

1963a: 196). The process repeats again and again, with states of relative confusion and emotional chaos recurring throughout life, as one feels all over again the absence of soul, mental disorientation, and loss of the center. One passes once more through the stages of looking, tracing, finding, capturing and taming the unruly unconscious with its complexes, instincts and compensatory and sometimes obstructive tendencies. In addition, there are more numinous experiences too and breakthroughs into the open. The repeated numinous experiences provide an increasingly stable marker in memory, as gradually a new and more whole personality gathers around this body of experience. Minding the self accumulates more psychic substance and permanence in consciousness. As the individuation process runs on, the personality matures around a center that is not only personal but also impersonal. This creates a sense of self that is not only ego-centered. As picture ten shows, the sage looks like a very ordinary man but clearly there is something different about him. A subtle sense of mystery surrounds him: "Making no use of secrets of the gods and wizards, he causes withered trees to bloom." He seems to bestow synchronistic effects on his environment, so something special emanates from him, but this is subtle and he takes no credit for it.

The Harvard psychologist, Henry Murray, wrote to his friend Jung in the 1950s and asked him to explain what he meant with the concept of individuation. He wanted to answer the question of his students: What does the individuated person look like? Jung replied: "The individuated human being is just ordinary and therefore almost invisible" (Jung 1975: 324). Jung continues and makes a reference to Zen Buddhism and to the work of D.T. Suzuki:

> As Zen Buddhism says: first mountains are mountains and the sea is the sea. Then mountains are no more mountains, the sea is no more the sea, and in the end the mountains will be the mountains and the sea will be the sea. Nobody can have a vision and not be changed by it. First he has no vision, and he is the man A, then he is himself plus a vision = the man B; and then it might be that the vision may influence his life, if he is not quite dull, and that is the man C.
>
> (Jung 1975: 324)

In picture ten we see, then, such a representative of individuation who looks quite ordinary and unnoticeable in a crowd, "dirty and dust-covered", but is somebody who has had a vision and has been changed by it. Mindful of the self, he is master of himself and his surroundings. He blesses the world and brings withered trees to bloom.

Note

1   I wish to thank Dr Paul Brutsche for introducing me to these beautiful paintings and also for his helpful psychological commentary on the series.

References

Alles G. (Ed.) (1996) *Rudolf Otto: Autobiographical and Social Essays*. Berlin and New York: Mouton de Gruyter

Ballin, U. (2002) 'Richard Wilhelm (1873-1930): Eine biographische Einführung', in Hirsch K. *Richard Wilhelm – Botschafter zweier Welten*. Frankfurt a.M.: Verlagsdruckerei Spengler

Borges, J.L. (1964) 'The God's script' in Yates D. A. Irby J. E. (Eds) *Labyrinths: Selected Stories and Other Writings*. New York: New Directions

Dubuisson, D. (2007) *The Western Construction of Religion*. Baltimore: Johns Hopkins Press

Erikson, E. (1969) *Gandhi's Truth*. New York: W.W. Norton & Company

Fingarette, H. (1972) *Confucius – The Secular as Sacred*. New York: Harper Torchbooks

Frankena, W. K. (1973) *Ethics*. Englewood Cliffs, NJ: Prentice-Hall

Freud, S. (1939) *Moses and Monotheism*, Jones K. (Trans.). London: Hogarth Press and the Institute of Psycho-analysis

Henderson, J. L. (2005) *Thresholds of Initiation*. Wilmette, IL: Chiron Publications

Hobson, J.A. (2002) *Dreaming: An Introduction to the Science of Sleep*. Oxford: Oxford University Press

Homans, P. (1995) *Jung in Context: Modernity and the Making of a Psychology* (2nd Ed.). Chicago, IL: University of Chicago Press

Jung, A. and Stiftung C.G. Jung. (2009) *The House of C.G. Jung*, with texts by Andreas Jung, Regula Michel, Arthur Rueegg, Judith Rohrer, Daniel Ganz. Wilmette, IL.: Chiron Publications

Jung, C.G. (1912) *Wandlungen und Symbole der Libido* Hinkle B. M. (Trans.) (1916) *Psychology of the Unconscious*. New York: Dodd, Mead and Co

—— (1912/1970) *Symbols of Transformation* in *The Collected Works* [CW] *of C.G. Jung* 5, Read H. Sir Fordham M. Adler G. (Eds). Bollingen Series XX. Princeton: Princeton University Press

—— (1916/1969) 'The transcendent function' in *CW* 8

—— (1921/1971) *Psychological Types* in *CW* 6

—— (1928/1966) 'The structure of the unconscious' in *CW* 7

—— (1929/1966) 'Problems of modern psychotherapy' in *CW* 16

—— (1931/1966) 'The practical use of dream analysis' in *CW* 16

—— (1933/1964) 'The meaning of psychology for modern man' in *CW* 10

—— (1930/1966) 'Richard Wilhelm: in memoriam' in *CW* 15

—— (1936/1964) 'Wotan' in *CW* 11

—— (1936/1969) *Psychology and Religion* in *CW* 11

—— (1938/1954) 'Psychological aspects of the mother archetype' in *CW* 9/i

—— (1938/1967) Foreword to the Second German Edition, 'Commentary on *The Secret of the Golden Flower*' in CW 13

—— (1940/1969) 'The psychology of the child archetype' in *CW* 9/i

—— (1941/1969) 'Psychological symbolism in the Mass' in *CW* 11

—— (1942/1969) 'A psychological approach to the Dogma of the Trinity' in *CW* 11

—— (1943/1966) *Two Essays in Analytical Psychology* in *CW* 7

—— (1944/1968) *Psychology and Alchemy* in *CW* 12

—— (1950/1968) *Aion: Researches into the Phenomenology of the Self* in *CW* 9ii

—— (1950/1969) 'Foreword to the *I Ching*' in *CW* 11

—— (1952/1969) 'Synchronicity: an acausal connecting principle' in *CW* 8

—— (1954/1969) *Answer to Job* in *CW* 11

—— (1955/1963) *Mysterium Coniunctionis* in *CW* 14

—— (1958/1964a) 'Flying saucers: a modern myth of things seen in the skies' in *CW* 10

—— (1958/1964b) 'A psychological view of conscience' in *CW* 10

—— (1963a) *Memories, Dreams, Reflections*. New York: Vintage Books

—— (1963b) 'Septem sermones ad mortuos' in *Memories, Dreams, Reflections*: (Appendix V, pp. 378–90). New York: Vintage Books

—— (1973) *C.G. Jung Letters Vol. 1: 1906-1950*, Adler G. Jaffé A. (Eds). Princeton: Princeton University Press

—— (1975) *C.G. Jung Letters Vol. 2: 1906-1950*, Adler G. Jaffé A. (Eds). Princeton: Princeton University Press

—— (1988) *Nietzsche's Zarathustra: Notes of the Seminar Given in 1934-1939*, Jarrett J. (Ed.). Princeton: Princeton University Press

—— (2009) *The Red Book*, S. Shamdasani (Ed.). New York: Norton

Jung, C.G. and Pauli, W. (1952/1955) *The Interpretation of Nature and the Psyche*. New York: Pantheon Books

Kapleau, R. P. (1980) *The Three Pillars of Zen*. New York: Anchor Books

Kenny, A. (1994) 'Descartes to Kant' in *The Oxford History of Western Philosophy*, Kenny A. (Ed.). Oxford: Oxford University Press

Kirsch, T. (1998) 'Jung and Tao'. *The Round Table Review*, Vol. VII, No. 3

Lammers A.C. Cunningham A. (eds) (2007) *The Jung-White Letters*, London and New York: Routledge

Lear, J. (2005) *Freud*. New York & London: Routledge

Neumann, E. (1949/1969) *Depth Psychology and a New Ethic*. New York: G.P. Putnam's Sons

Ogden, T. (1999) *Reverie and Interpretation*. London: Karnac Books

Otto, R. (1917/1950) *Das Heilige*. Munich: C.H. Beck Harvey J. W. (Trans.) (1923; 2nd Ed. 1950) *The Idea of the Holy*. Oxford: Oxford University

Rennstich, K. (1998) 'Richard Wilhelm' in *Biographish-Bibliographisches Kirchenlexikon*, Band XIII (1998). Nordhausen, Germany: Verlag Traugott Bautz

Rizzuto, A-M. (1998) *Why Did Freud Reject God?* New Haven: Yale University Press

Robinson J. M. (Ed.) (1988) *The Nag Hammadi Library*. San Francisco: Harper and Row

Schildmann, W. (1991/2006) *Karl Barths Träume: Zur verborgenen Psychodynamik seines Werkes*. Zürich: Theologisher Verlag Zürich

Schwartz, R. (2004) 'Introduction' in Schwartz R. (Ed.) *Transcendence: Philosophy, Literature, and Theology Approach the Beyond*. New York & London: Routledge

Solomon, H. (2004) 'The ethical attitude in analytic training and practice' in Cambray J. Carter L. (Eds). *Analytical Psychology: Contemporary Perspectives in Jungian Analysis*. Hove and New York: Routledge

Stein, M. (1995) 'Synchronicity and divine providence' in Spiegelman M. (Ed.) *Protestantism and Jungian Psychology*. Tempe, Arizona: New Falcon Publications

—— (1998) *Transformation: Emergence of the Self*. College Station: Texas A & M University Press

—— (1998) *Jung's Map of the Soul: An Introduction*. Chicago: Open Court

—— (2003) 'The role of Victor White in C.G. Jung's writings'. The Guild of Pastoral Psychology, Guild Lecture No. 285

—— (2006) *The Principle of Individuation*. Wilmette, IL.: Chiron Publications

Strand, M. (2005) 'My name'. *The New Yorker*, April 11 2005, p. 68

Tacey, D. (2004) *The Spirituality Revolution: The Emergence of Contemporary Spirituality*. Hove and New York: Brunner-Routledge

—— (2008) 'Imagining transcendence at the end of modernity' in Huskinson L. (ed.) *Dreaming the Myth Onwards: New Directions in Jungian Therapy and Thought*. London: Routledge

Tillich, P. (1967) 'The holy — The absolute and the relative in religion' in *My Search for Absolutes*. New York: Simon and Shuster

Yerushalmi, Y. H. (1991) *Freud's Moses: Judaism Terminable and Interminable*. New Haven and London: Yale University Press

Index

An environmentally friendly book printed and bound in England by www.printondemand-worldwide.com

PEFC Certified

This product is
from sustainably
managed forests
and controlled
sources

www.pefc.org

PEFC/16-33-415

This book is made of chain-of-custody materials; FSC materials for the cover and PEFC materials for the text pages.

#0204 - 290416 - C0 - 234/156/8 - PB - 9780415377843